Of Mice and Men

JOHN STEINBECK

Guide written by
Stewart Martin

A *Letts* *EXPLORE* **Literature Guide**

First published 1994
Reprinted 1994, 1995, 1997 twice, 1998 twice, 1999, 2000, 2001
This edition revised by Ron Simpson

Letts Educational,
The Chiswick Centre.
414 Chiswick High Road,
London W4 5TF
Tel: 020 8996 3333

Text © John Mahoney and Stewart Martin 1994

Typeset by Jordan Publishing Design

Self-test questions devised by Hilary Lissenden

Text design Jonathan Barnard

Cover and text illustrations Hugh Marshall

Graphic illustration Ian Foulis and Associates, Barbara Linton

Design © Letts Educational Ltd

Acknowledgements
Extracts from *Of Mice and Men* by John Steinbeck published by William Heinemann are reprinted by kind permission of Reed International Books.

Examination questions reproduced by kind permission of the Northern Examination and Assessment Board.

The answers supplied to the Exam Board questions are solely the responsibility of the author, and are not supplied or approved by the Exam Boards.

British Library Cataloguing in Publication Data
A CIP record for this book is available from the British Library

ISBN 1 85758 264 0

Printed and bound in Great Britain
Ashford Colour Press, Gosport, Hampshire

Letts Educational Ltd, a division of Granada Learning Ltd. Part of the Granada Media Group.

Contents

Plot synopsis

The story is set in California in the 1930s during the Great Depression and features as its main characters two itinerant (wandering) farm workers called George and Lennie. George is small, quick and intelligent, while Lennie is, by contrast, a slow, simple-minded giant who has a passion for 'petting' things – especially mice, rabbits and other soft, silky things. Because he does not know his own strength, he often 'pets' these creatures to death. George and Lennie travel around together in search of work, and George takes care of Lennie, who is innocent of the world and its ways. They have a dream of a place of their own – a small ranch where they can live and work for themselves. They are currently on the run from the town of Weed, where Lennie caused trouble by innocently fondling a girl's dress. They travel to a ranch where they have work and meet Candy, an old, crippled worker. Curley, the son of the ranch boss, turns out to be an aggressive and threatening man who frightens Lennie and worries George. Curley is always searching for his attractive young wife, who dislikes him and spends a lot of her time giving the ranch-hands 'the eye' in a seductive way. In spite of his misgivings about the situation, George decides that they will stay because they need the work and the money. Candy overhears them talking about their 'dream farm' and offers to put in his savings if they will let him join them. Lennie is given a puppy by Slim, the senior ranch-hand. Curley starts a fight with Lennie, who crushes his hand in self-defence. Lennie tells the black stable buck, Crooks, about their 'dream farm' and he too expresses a wish to be involved. They are interrupted by Curley's wife, who has guessed that it was Lennie who beat Curley and begins to take an interest in him. She contrives to meet him when he is by himself in the barn and he is feeling frightened and guilty because he has accidentally killed his puppy whilst petting it. She invites him to stroke her hair but becomes upset by his roughness. Unnerved by her screams, Lennie tries to quieten her, accidentally breaking her neck and killing her. He runs away and the other ranch-hands set out in pursuit, but George, knowing where to find him, forces himself to kill Lennie with a shot in the back of the head.

■ About John Steinbeck

Much of *Of Mice And Men* is based upon Steinbeck's life and experiences. He was born in 1902 at Salinas in California and graduated from Salinas High School in 1919. He went on to study English at Stanford but left without getting a degree.

In the years that followed, he had many casual jobs, varying from newspaper work to itinerant ranch-hand. He had some local success as a writer, before *Of Mice And Men* (originally called 'Something that Happened') became an immediate and worldwide success and brought him international recognition. The publication of the novel was followed in the same year (1937) by a stageplay, which won an award for the best New York play. Steinbeck's established readers would not have been surprised that his book had as its background agricultural labour in California, as he had already become known as a writer interested in contemporary issues.

In the novel Steinbeck highlights a social problem of immense proportions and of which he had experience at first hand. Climatic changes in the West of America between 1880 and 1930 resulted in the destruction through drought of large tracts of fertile land which had supported the early homesteaders. These were settlers who had established the sort of small farms that represent the 'promised joy' of the workers in the story. They were driven from the land by the 'great American dust bowl' that resulted from these shifts in climate plus over-farming of the land. The great financial collapse of 1929 which heralded the Depression increased unemployment and poverty throughout the United States. White-collar and industrial workers suffered heavily, but for those who sought a living on farms the situation was doubly disastrous. Franklin D. Roosevelt's New Deal economics did much to reduce the problem, but in 1937 it was a long way from disappearing and would not fully do so until America's entry into World War II in 1941.

As a result itinerant American workers replaced the traditional immigrant Mexican labour in South-Western states like California. They were exploited by farm owners, who employed them on low rates of pay and in appalling conditions. These men were only in demand for short periods at a time, and they had to save enough from seasonal work, such as harvesting crops and fruits, to support them through the rest of the year. Because of their solitary lifestyle, and their extreme mobility, little could be done to organise their welfare through trade-union membership. This was of great concern to

Steinbeck, who dealt with this problem in his novel *In Dubious Battle*, and also in his most successful book *The Grapes of Wrath*, which won the Pulitzer Prize in 1940.

John Steinbeck's novels of this time had therefore a grittily realistic element and also a political slant: his undoubted masterpiece, *The Grapes of Wrath*, strongly supports Roosevelt's state interference to reduce unemployment and even reveals Communist sympathies. However, the other main influence on Steinbeck was quite different: all his life he had an uncritical devotion to the Arthurian legend. Nobility and honour are venerated, as in the Knights of the Round Table, and many of his characters are on a quest, as for the Holy Grail. There are even hints of the noble company of knights errant in Lennie and George travelling together in pursuit of a dream, and the Joad family doing likewise in *The Grapes of Wrath*. The poetic element in *Of Mice and Men* stems from Steinbeck's love of the legends of King Arthur.

John Steinbeck was one of the finest and most successful of American novelists. Deservedly popular in schools are *The Red Pony* (1938) and *The Pearl* (1948). His most ambitious and most impressive post-war novel was a powerful family saga, *East of Eden* (1952), that, like *Of Mice and Men* and *The Grapes of Wrath*, was made into an outstanding film. However, when he received the Nobel Prize for Literature in 1962, it was specifically for his pre-war novels.

John Steinbeck died in 1969, America's most distinguished novelist, but it would be fair to say that, for all his later success, his finest work came in his realistic/poetic response to the sufferings of the American working-man some 30 years earlier.

George

George

George is quick-witted and intelligent. His vigilance and nervous caution are in part derived from his endurance of physical hardship in the past. George has a good working knowledge of farming and ranching. His love for the stillness and harmony of the countryside gives weight to his dream of owning and working a small farm. He is very keen to change the monotony of his present situation. He is aware of the low expectations and aimless lifestyle that are typical of the average itinerant farm-worker.

George has taken on responsibility for Lennie partly out of pity, partly out of affection and partly for companionship. He has the strength of mind and character to carry out the compassionate killing of Lennie in the final chapter.

In many ways, George and Lennie are the two incomplete halves of one whole, contented person – where one of them is strong the other one is weak. They are in some ways similar in appearance too – even down to the way they move and walk. Lennie is in many ways George's 'shadow'. George represents the head or intelligence of the pair, whilst Lennie's nature is intensely physical – he is the body. Seeing the two characters this way shows you the error of assuming that George is in some way exploiting Lennie, as the boss suspects. We are, however, prevented from seeing their relationship in merely sentimental terms because of the practical realism which George shows. George understands that Lennie is both a hindrance and an advantage to him, and his feelings for him never become sentimental or mawkish.

However, George is not entirely blameless for the disastrous end which befalls Lennie. He knows how Lennie tends to behave and when they arrive at the ranch he senses undercurrents that could lead to disaster. George ignores these danger signals as his need for a 'stake' outweighs his natural caution. For one night he even leaves the vulnerable

Lennie behind, in spite of the problems at the ranch, and this leads to Lennie's downfall.

Lennie

Lennie

Although in many ways Lennie is very child-like, he also shows signs of adult maturity. Despite his terror of violence he is a man of great physical strength. He is frequently described in terms of an animal, suggesting not only his bear-like tendency to hold onto his prey and inflict great damage, but also a kind of animal innocence. Lennie has no awareness of any kind of morality – which means that the ordinary values of 'good' or 'bad' are difficult to attribute to him. Lennie's obsession for 'petting' shows that he has deep-rooted emotional needs which he himself may not understand, but which nevertheless have to be satisfied. There is a dreadful progression in his victims from dead mouse to dead girl. Lennie's irresistible urge to 'pet' collides with the desires and sexuality of Curley's wife.

Some critics have detected a definite semi-religious echo running through the book. At the opening of the novel Lennie is characterised by naivety and innocence; by the end he has fallen from grace (he has committed murder) and by this act has deprived himself of the paradise of the 'dream farm'. There seems no way he can escape 'retribution'. Do you agree with this? How far is Lennie ever really innocent? Certainly he often seems to be ignorant of the consequences of his actions and never seems to learn from them. Is Lennie innocent, mentally retarded, or both?

Crooks

Crooks

Crooks is a literate black cripple who tends horses on the ranch. He has long been the victim of oppressive violence and prejudice and has retired behind a facade of aloofness and reserve, his natural personality deadened and suppressed by years of antagonism. He has known better times and, unlike most Southern blacks at that time, was brought up on a smallholding run by his father. This is the type of home longed for by Lennie, George and Candy and, despite his initial cynicism, Crooks also becomes caught up in their dream of escape. Crooks' automatic rejection of friendship or companionship has more to do with the anguish of his loneliness than with anything else. Once encouraged to do so, he reveals that he has an intelligent awareness of life. He has thought hard during his long hours of solitude. His new-found confidence and self-respect encourage him to try to counter the intrusion of Curley's wife, but he is humiliated by her vicious threats. His new optimism is finally defeated by George's dismissive attitude to the suggestion that he might participate in the running of the 'dream farm'.

Curley

Curley

Curley is a small man and seems to have developed an inferiority complex as a result. He is continually aggressive and constantly looking for an opportunity to assert his masculinity. Humiliated by his wife's apparent dissatisfaction and unhappiness, Curley needs to boost his self-esteem and confidence. His stance is that of a professional fighter – he was once a boxer – but, significantly, he fights unfairly. He takes advantage of those whom he thinks are weak, whilst carefully avoiding those he considers to be a match for him. He takes pleasure in inflicting the maximum amount of damage and pain possible, to dispel his frustration and anger and maintain his authority through violence. Even his approach to intimacy is crude and physical, symbolised by his glove which, according to Candy, is full of vaseline.

Curley's wife

Curley's wife

Curley's wife is never named in the novel: even the way she is referred to – Curley's wife – makes her sound like Curley's possession. She is not treated as an individual in her own right – which is something she bitterly resents – but is seen by various characters as a symbol of other things – a temptress, a chattel, a sex-object, or a piece of 'jail bait'. Although she is married, she flaunts herself around the ranch in inappropriate clothing, flirting with the ranch-hands. She seems very conscious of the effect this has on the men. She seems preoccupied with strategies which will help her avoid detection by her husband so that she can be in private with the ranch-hands if that is what they wish. She manages this by pretending always to be looking for Curley!

She has dreams of a better, more fulfilling life, but these are based on glossy film magazines and the easy promises of men she has known in the past. Her ambition to work in films or in the music hall stems from her desire to be admired. This wish is partly rooted in vanity and partly in her insecurity and loneliness, much of which is brought about by her husband's inadequacies and fault-finding behaviour. We do not know how far she would pursue her assignations with the men if she were given the chance, and we have only the ranch-hands' speculations about this as evidence. Our only opportunity to find out occurs in her meeting with Lennie in the barn, and this is described with very skilful ambiguity by Steinbeck. Certainly her general posture and conduct is full of sensual promise. Although her panic at Lennie's petting of her hair leads to her death, this could have been caused just as easily by Lennie's unthinking roughness as by any decision on her part that things had gone too far.

Slim

Slim

Slim is dignified and charismatic and a master craftsman. He exerts a natural authority with a gentleness and friendliness that contrasts with the pervasive violence that shapes the lives of the other characters. In times of conflict or stress it is to Slim that the ranch-hands turn. His magnanimous tolerance of the shortcomings of others is shown in the care he exhibits for all who need his attention and support. He has great perception and an intuitive sense of justice. He represents a strong moral force in the novel, and acts almost like a 'conscience' to other characters.

Steinbeck's descriptions of Slim suggest an idealised characterisation, though Slim's own words and actions are convincingly realistic. Steinbeck attaches images of royalty and divinity to him: in the paragraph when he is first mentioned, the words 'majesty', 'royalty', 'prince' and 'authority' are all applied to him.

Candy

Candy is near to the end of his useful life on the farm and knows he has little to look forward to. The loss of his hand stresses the casual violence of the ranch-workers' lives. He also loses his dog – the only companionship he has enjoyed. But he is given renewed comfort, strength and self-respect by the prospect of a part-ownership of the dream farm with Lennie and George. Just as he realistically measures his own prospects for the future, he predicts a grim end for Lennie at the hands of the mob.

Carlson

Carlson is practical and unsentimental and takes pride in his gun and his ability with it. Carlson's actions are never totally objectionable: his continual complaints about Candy's dog may be inconsiderate, but he has a case and he spares Candy by doing the job for him (and takes a spade, as Slim advises). However, we usually see him in aggressive situations, though we support him in facing down Curley. At the end he has no understanding of the feelings of George and Slim on the death of Lennie.

The boss

The boss appears only once and, though his manner is not notably pleasant, he is described as 'pretty good' by George and 'a nice fella' by Candy: no doubt there are worse, though Candy adds, 'You got to take him right.' His manner is aggressive and he is at pains to prove that he is something better than a labouring man (the boots and spurs, all the business with book and pencil), but his treatment of George and Lennie seems fair.

Themes and images in *Of Mice and Men*

> **Themes** are the important ideas that run through the book. You will come across them lots of times. They connect together the story, the characters and the different scenes in the book.
>
> When words and descriptions suggest a picture in your mind, that is called an **image**. Images are often used to make an idea stronger, or to encourage you to think of things from a particular point of view. If you described someone as being 'as thin as a rake' or as behaving 'like a wild animal' you would be using simple examples of images. Read the following notes carefully.

Authority

Authority

Various forms of authority are present in the novel – from the God-like authority of Slim to the ineffectual bullying of Curley. The boss's authority is, like his dress, black and severe and is based on exploitation. George's authority over Lennie is more difficult to classify; it has elements of the same authority which Candy has over his dog, but sometimes Lennie is able to reverse its action, as when he threatens to run away.

Several characters use violence or financial power as the basis of their authority, whilst others seem to have authority because they avoid exploitation. Generally, those who use violence or financial power are unable to understand the values and drives of those who do not. For example, Carlson and Curley cannot fathom the distress of Slim and George at the end of the novel.

Dreams

Dreams

Many of the characters in the novel have dreams, in the sense that they have hopes or ambitions. These dreams are often kept secret to begin with. George is displeased when he discovers that Lennie and Candy have told Crooks about their secret 'dream farm'. In contrast, Curley's wife seems almost desperate to tell Lennie about her dreams. It is ironic that she confides in someone who appears to have no interest in, or understanding of, what she is saying.

Many of the workers have dreams of one kind or another, and sometimes they share the same dream. Generally speaking, there is a choice of two types of dream open to them: the dream that includes companionship, honesty and love (like the 'dream farm' idea) or the dream (more like a nightmare, really) of a solitary state that excludes all other human contact. The 'dream farm' represents ambition and the possibility of escape from the itinerant workers' loneliness and poverty. George's vision is an example of the second kind of unhappy vision, when he sees his future as unending aimless drifting: 'I'll take my fifty bucks an' I'll stay all night in some lousy cat house. Or I'll set in some pool-room till ever'body goes home.'

Loneliness

Loneliness

Many of the characters are lonely and this motivates them to look for an alternative way of life. This is one of the reasons why they are drifters: they are continually searching, often without knowing what they are really looking for. Characters are also lonely because of something within themselves, something which almost seems to make their loneliness inevitable. Different characters seek comfort and solace in different things – for Candy it is his dog; for George and Lennie it is each other; for Crooks it is his pride and his unerring skill at pitching horseshoes.

Nature

Nature

The world of nature plays a large part in the events of the novel. Lennie is described as a 'bear', and is often surrounded by animals (especially the small animals which he 'pets') and the natural environment. Lennie is himself very 'natural' in that he has an animal-like simplicity and innocence. The ranch-hands' lives are unnatural because they lead a rootless existence outside of any 'proper' society. They are like men adrift in a wilderness.

The behaviour of human beings towards animals is echoed by the way the characters behave towards each other. Candy's dog is at the end of its useful life and its killing is justified by some of the men because of this. If judged in the same kind of way, the killing of Lennie may seem to be justified.

Steinbeck also uses animals set in their natural world as a way of reinforcing another main theme in the book, violence – as when a snake appears at the start of the book and another which appears at the end is killed. Nature is also shown to be full of powerful spiritual forces. For example, near the start of the book, the large carp 'sank mysteriously into the dark water again'.

Violence

Violence

The world of the men in the book is filled with unnecessary and gratuitous violence. The boss is a good example of this in the way he treats the men and permits fighting. Curley is another good example, with his almost completely irrational aggressiveness – as George remarks at their first meeting: 'Say, what the hell's he got on his shoulder?' Carlson is another character who seems to thrive on violence either when he is arguing with others or when he is goading them on. The gun's easy availability – together with Carlson's unthinking but detailed explanation of his killing technique – provides George with the means to dispatch Lennie later on. As you read the book, try to identify exactly why you think each violent character behaves in the way he does.

Examiner's tip icon

This icon is used to draw attention to a section of the **Text commentary** that is particularly relevant to the titles considered in **How to write an examination essay**. Each time it is used, a note adds a comment or piece of advice.

■ Text commentary

Section 1

On their way from the town of Weed, George and Lennie spend the night by a natural pool in a valley, before travelling on to the ranch.

Evening of a hot day...

The book opens with the suggestion that the peaceful world of nature is

Nature

disturbed by man. This becomes more pronounced during this section as the 'sound of footsteps' grows louder and the animals flee to safety. This movement from harmony to discord appears in most of the natural settings in the book. You should pay careful attention to the way nature is described. For example, here the green pool is portrayed as an idyllic and beautiful place which is innocent and peaceful, rather like the Garden of Eden. How are the two different atmospheres created by Steinbeck?

The opening descriptions of each section are a particular feature of the novel; in your essays you need to see them as more than just background. Idyllic descriptions like this help to create some sense of hope and optimism (see question 1 on page 61).

George and Lennie make their first appearance

George and Lennie are itinerant (wandering) workers. They are drifters who move from ranch to ranch. They dress in the traditional manner of cowboys, from whom they descend. They are skilled in the various aspects of farm work.

George

George

George – 'every part of him defined' – gives an immediate impression of intelligence. He is reminiscent of a quick-witted animal by his 'restless' ways. George leads the pair and we can see that he is clearly the one who is in charge. Both men have endured much physical hardship. George washes in the pool in traditional cowboy style. Unlike Lennie, he is a cautious type of person.

Lennie

Lennie

Lennie is described as a 'bear'. This 'animal' context establishes at once the essential nature of the man – the combination of brute strength and animal-like innocence. The bear is a particularly appropriate image for Lennie, because it shares not only his harmless appearance (as of a teddy-bear), but also his tendency to hold onto things in his 'bear-hug'. In the case of both creatures, very few survive such gestures of affection. Steinbeck suggests a great deal about Lennie by describing his movements.

Lennie has a drink

Nature

The unthinking way Lennie drinks from the 'green' pool reinforces the impression of a markedly animal temperament. Lennie's animal-like innocence is emphasised when he is compared to a horse. Like an animal, Lennie always tries to satisfy his immediate needs and seems unable to see the possible consequences. In this case, George reminds him it was only the previous night that he was sick.

Bad omens

One of Lennie's most dangerous failings is his inability to learn from past experience. George's admonishment establishes his role as Lennie's mentor (or keeper), with the responsibility of protecting Lennie from himself. Why do you think George is ill at ease and apprehensive here? It may have something to do with the way Lennie behaves when he is ill.

Lennie and George 'suit' each other because of their complementary natures. Both men are dressed the same way, but in temperament they are different – Lennie is slow, clumsy, and 'easy-going' where George is quick, precise, apprehensive and cautious. Notice that it is Lennie who seems always to suffer because of his impetuous and reckless behaviour.

Some aspects of Lennie's behaviour contribute to the humour in the novel.

Nature

Here, for example, the way he dips 'his whole head under, hat and all' is contrasted with George's behaviour. This reveals George's awareness that the open countryside is not without its dangers; he knows that 'You never oughta drink water when it ain't running'. This episode reinforces our impression of Lennie as being more like an animal than a man. Look at how he uses his 'paw'.

Lennie sits just like George does

Not only is George Lennie's mentor, but clearly Lennie 'looks up' to him as a model of correct behaviour, and tries to please George with his actions.

The exposition: George and Lennie

The exposition (account of events before the story proper) puts the relationship between George and Lennie into a slightly wider context. For example, if they are treated in a disdainful and casual way by an ordinary working person such as a bus driver, then their status must be quite low. This may then give you a clue about why George actually needs to care for Lennie. Do you think George needs Lennie as much as Lennie needs George? Lennie may not in fact just be a natural, innocent, animal-like creature: he may have considerable human dignity of his own. Look carefully at the George-Lennie relationship as you read the text and try to see why it is that they stay together and what exactly it is that each of them puts into and gets out of their relationship.

"Where we goin', George?"

Lennie

Lennie is not able to remember things easily. Steinbeck uses this to provide us with background material and moves the narrative forward gently. We are told something about what caused the two men to be on the run from their last employment and this is the first suggestion that Lennie's animal-like behaviour includes an unconscious, instinctive search for affection.

Lennie thinks he has lost his work card

This episode follows Lennie's 'delighted smile' when he remembers 'some girls'. This and Lennie's 'petting' of small animals tells you about his need for some sort of physical contact. This is an important aspect of Lennie's character – one that is tragically resolved at the end of the book. As the novel unfolds, notice how Lennie's fatal petting of other creatures progresses from a dead mouse to hoped-for rabbits, to a puppy, and finally to Curley's wife.

George demands the mouse

Authority

George's shout 'Give it here' demonstrates the need for forceful authority to control Lennie. George changes from a companion-figure to a parent-figure as he reprimands Lennie for his child-like behaviour. How far does it also seem like a relationship between master and animal?

George and Lennie can be seen as the two halves of one complete individual. From a psychological point of view, George is the rational one who is in control of the 'whole individual', while Lennie is the one full of basic animal desires or 'earth longings', as Steinbeck calls them.

Steinbeck stresses the variety of mood in the relationship between George and Lennie. George moves very quickly from stern firmness to trying to instil good behaviour in Lennie by kinder means. This emphasises the child-like response of Lennie.

When they meet the boss, Lennie is "Jus' gonna stan' there."

Violence

First Steinbeck revealed some past trouble with 'girls', and now we find that the two men have recently been hounded from their previous jobs as Lennie has done 'bad things'. The fact that Lennie 'giggled' at the thought of it makes the incident sound less serious than it really was, but in fact he had a close shave with death. This is excellent narrative technique to hold the reader's interest; Steinbeck is gradually revealing to us the enormity of the event and its consequences.

George thinks that without Lennie he could "live so easy and maybe have a girl"

Dreams

This is the first example in the book of characters dreaming of better things in the future. Such dreams become increasingly important. Why then does George remain with Lennie if he thinks life could be so much better without him?

It is easy to see why Lennie stays with George and also to identify what he wants from life. In many essay titles you need to form an opinion on the more difficult reverse question: what does George want, and why?

The Gabilan mountains flame with the light of the setting sun

Nature

George appreciates the stillness and harmony of the pastoral scene around them. This moment of calm interrupts the interplay of the two characters, before the 'parental' side of the relationship is reintroduced by Lennie's petulant demand for ketchup with his beans.

This pastoral interlude links up with the opening of the novel and re-establishes a sense of harmony. It also introduces a gentler tone. We are encouraged to see the world of nature as an innocent child might. Lennie desperately needs something to pet. He is prepared to hunt around for the carcass of the mouse and is evasive and guilty when George orders him to hand it over.

"What mouse, George? I ain't got no mouse."

Lennie

Steinbeck again uses animal imagery to describe Lennie as being 'like a terrier'. They both share a determination to hold on to things. This prepares us for events to come. Lennie is reluctant to let go of the mouse, which he has accidentally 'broken' by petting it. He has killed other small creatures, or 'pinched their heads a little', as he puts it. He wants something that is warm and alive. Lennie's behaviour will have devastating consequences in the future.

Half-darkness falls on the scene

The flow of the narrative is interrupted again by a piece of pastoral description that restores peace and harmony. There is a powerful sense of hidden things starting to emerge – as in the way the 'big carp' rises, then sinks 'mysteriously', leaving 'widening rings' similar to those created by Lennie's 'paw' earlier. This image of widening rings hints at the increasing repercussions of Lennie's actions and suggests that Lennie has mysterious or subconscious depths.

Nature

George loses his temper with Lennie about the ketchup

George's frustrations with Lennie's behaviour come to a head at this point. Steinbeck now reveals the destructiveness of Lennie's actions. Lennie is completely unaware of the basic desires and drives that prompt his actions. He does not understand how his 'innocent' gestures are interpreted by others.

George

The better life which George says he could enjoy if he did not have Lennie seems a fairly limited one: drink, food, hired women and gambling. It is the very lifestyle that the other workers find so unsatisfying. By staying with Lennie, George actually enjoys companionship and a sense of responsibility – rewards that are greater than the empty experience of the common itinerant worker about whom George keeps talking. This is why, in spite of all his complaining, George does not strike off on his own.

It is obvious why George finds Lennie occasionally irritating. However, Steinbeck uses various methods to endear Lennie to the reader. He appears completely without malice or evil; his innocence echoes the purity of the surrounding world of nature. How do you think Steinbeck achieves this? You should look at the imagery with which he is usually associated, and also the reactions other than irritation that he inspires in George.

Of Mice and Men is, as a story, short and simple, but the characters are presented subtly. Lennie could be described as a homicidal half-wit: you need to consider the various ways in which Steinbeck makes us reject that view and find goodness in him.

Soledad

Loneliness

George and Lennie find themselves a 'few miles south of Soledad'. This is a real place in California and its name – which is Spanish – can mean loneliness or a lonely place. George describes himself and Lennie as the sort of people who 'are the loneliest guys in the world'. Although the boss of the ranch thinks that George exploits Lennie, all the ranch-hands come to see that the reason for their relationship is mutual loneliness.

Lennie says he will go off in the hills

The fact that George 'looked ashamedly at the flames' tells you that he is sorry for the pain he has caused Lennie by his outburst. Lennie 'slowly and cautiously' crawls round the fire with the wariness of a wild animal.

Nature

George

Lennie suggests that he could go off into the hills on his own and leave George. This is what a wild animal might do. Living in a cave and lying in the sun is particularly appropriate for a bear, the most dominant animal image so far. Lennie has a strange kind of animal intellect – an intelligence based on intuition. Of course Lennie's suggestion is not welcomed by George, not only because Lennie would not survive (or would he?), but because George, despite his fits of temper, actually needs Lennie. George gets physical protection, a feeling of doing something worthwhile in looking after Lennie and a boost to his own self-esteem because Lennie makes him feel superior. Notice that George also finds an excuse for his own failure to make a success of himself, and later admits this to Slim when he confesses: 'I ain't so bright neither'.

This section where Lennie offers to leave George points out various of the key elements in their relationship. You would find it of great use in question 2, page 62: George's responsibility and caring for others, Lennie's inability to survive freedom, etc.

After Lennie has killed Curley's wife, George retains little interest in the 'dream farm'. This is because the farm is a symbol of the companionship and comfort that he is searching for in his life, not an end in itself. The farm would be meaningless if he were there alone. The relationship between George and Lennie is very important to George. They are not actually related, but George later tells the boss that Lennie is his 'cousin'. Do the other characters in the novel also protect and care for each other?

George tries to make amends to Lennie for his outburst

Lennie has gained the initiative with his threat to move into a cave and George seems to sense a danger to himself. By way of compensation for his outburst, George offers Lennie a puppy – not knowing that it will contribute to his later downfall. It is characteristic of the role of fate in the novel that the best intentions of people produce adverse effects. With hindsight, there seems to be a tragic inevitability in the way that these separate strands of incident and words spoken are carefully and unerringly woven together. This pervades the climax of the story.

Lennie avoids the bait

George comments to Lennie that, if he goes off on his own, "Somebody'd shoot you as a coyote". It is ironic that in the end it is George who shoots Lennie in the same way Candy's old dog is shot by Carlson. Steinbeck weaves his ideas very closely together and sometimes casual remarks later turn out to carry the weight of the whole narrative. Here they contribute to a gathering sense of doom. In attempting to keep Lennie from harm, George ironically contributes to his subsequent downfall.

George again tells Lennie the story how it is with them

Lennie enjoys George's story just as a child enjoys a familiar fairy story. But
 it represents far more to both men. The 'paradise' or 'heaven', as Crooks later calls it, becomes not only *their* dream, but also that of Candy, Crooks and Curley's wife. After killing Curley's wife, Lennie is tormented by the certainty that he has destroyed his chances of ever reaching this 'paradise'.

Dreams   Lennie and George are complementary characters and their relationship has a symmetry about it. George has experience, wisdom and intelligence and can use these to look after Lennie. Lennie, although limited by his simple intellect, has size and immense strength. Lennie is therefore welcome at ranches because of his capacity for work. He is also a useful deterrent should anybody wish to take advantage of George's lack of stature. The expression that Lennie uses here – "because I got you…and you got me" is a very accurate assessment of their need for each other.

Beans for supper

 The small detail of the few beans slipping out of the side of Lennie's mouth reminds us again of Lennie's childlike behaviour.

George briefs Lennie on what he is to say when they reach the farm and tells him to return to this place and hide in the
Lennie   brush if he gets into trouble. When this actually happens, it

completes the symmetry of the novel. This is particularly appropriate because of the way the pool has been described as a natural haven, a secret dream-like place which is a natural sanctuary for Lennie. Bear in mind that in the Bible, Adam took refuge in a similar way from the wrath of God.

Nature

Lennie would like different-coloured rabbits on their farm

The first episode of the novel ends on a note of peace and harmony as the two men drift off to sleep. This adds to the natural kinship that exists between Lennie and George.

■ Self-test questions Section 1

Uncover the plot

Delete two of the three alternatives given, to find the correct plot. Beware possible misconceptions and muddles.

Two errant/itinerant/eminent farm hands, George and Lennie, camp beside a natural pool in a valley before travelling on to a nearby ranch to find work/buy a house/live off the land. It becomes clear that George – small and shapeless/quick-witted/pale-eyed – is responsible for the huge and nervous/restless/child-like Lennie, and that the two men have had to leave the town of Salinas/Soledad/Weed because Lennie unwittingly frightened a girl/mouse/rabbit there. George expresses his pride/resentment/shame at having to look after Lennie, but when Lennie offers to give him his mouse/shoot himself/leave him, he regrets his meanness. We learn that Lennie has a passion for 'petting' pretty things, especially girls/dresses/small animals, unaware of his own dangerous strength. George describes their dream of giving up work/buying a house/finding permanent work on a ranch; he tells Lennie to return to Weed/the pool/the ranch if he should get into any trouble.

Who? Why? What? When? Where? How?

1   Where is the pool beside which George and Lennie spend the night?
2   What evidence is there that other men have camped there?
3   Why does George scold Lennie for drinking from the pool?
4   After drinking, what does Lennie do?
5   What does Lennie have in his pocket, and what doesn't he have in his pocket?
6   Who was the 'lady' that used to give Lennie mice?
7   Why did Lennie and George have to leave Weed?
8   According to them, why are Lennie and George different from the other ranch workers?
9   What do the two of them plan to do, and what do they need to succeed?
10   Why does George tell Lennie not to say a word on their arrival at the ranch?

Who is this?

1   Who is '...small and quick, dark of face, with restless eyes and sharp, strong features'?
2   Who is '...a huge man, (who) walked heavily, dragging his feet a little, the way a bear drags his paws'?

3　What '…drank with long gulps, snorting into the water like a horse'?
4　Whose head is 'held up like a periscope'?
5　Who 'jerked back' and 'yelled'?
6　Who are 'the loneliest guys in the world'?
7　Who is going to 'live off the fatta the lan', and what does that mean?

Who said that?

1　Who says: 'Poor bastard,' of whom, and why?
2　Who says: '…if I was alone I could live so easy'?
3　Who says: 'It ain't the same if I tell it', of what, and why do you think it isn't the same?

A complicated friendship

The author reveals the nature of the friendship between the two men gradually, both through action and through dialogue. Comment on what aspect or aspects of the characters and relationship are revealed in the following lines.

1　'They had walked in single file down the path, and even in the open one stayed behind the other.'
2　' "You never had none, you crazy bastard. I got both of 'em here. Think I'd let you carry your own work card?" '
3　'He heard Lennie's big whimpering cry and wheeled about. "Blubberin' like a baby? Jesus Christ! A big guy like you." Lennie's lip quivered and tears started in his eyes. "Aw, Lennie!" George put his hand on Lennie's shoulder. "I ain't takin' it away jus' for meanness…" '
4　'Lennie avoided the bait. He had sensed his advantage. "If you don't want me, you only jus' got to say so, and I'll go off in those hills right there – right up in those hills and live by myself. An' I won't get no mice stole from me." '
5　'Lennie broke in. "But not us! Because… because I got you to look after me, and you got me to look after you, and that's why." He laughed delightedly.'

Important images

What effect(s) do you think the author is trying to achieve by using the following images/symbols?

1　'On the sand-banks the rabbits sat as quietly as little grey, sculptured stones.'
2　'Lennie dabbled his big paw in the water and wiggled his fingers so the water arose in little splashes: rings widened across the pool…'
3　'Only the tops of the Gabilan mountains flamed with the light of the sun that had gone from the valley.'
4　'A big carp rose to the surface of the pool, gulped air, and then sunk mysteriously into the dark water again…'
5　'Slowly, like a terrier who doesn't want to bring a ball to its master, Lennie approached, drew back, approached again.'

Section 2

Lennie and George arrive at the ranch. Curley takes a dislike to Lennie. Carlson suggests that Slim should give one of his dog's puppies to Candy, and that Candy's old dog should be put down.

The setting of the bunkhouse is probably derived from Steinbeck's own experience as a ranch-hand. As with the novel's opening description, the technique is theatrical, setting the scene first and then introducing characters through dialogue. This 'home' for the workers is very sparse in comforts and contrasts strongly with the richness of nature described in the novel's opening section.

"The boss was expectin' you last night..."

Authority

This opening remark establishes the character of the boss before we meet him. We feel unease at such an immediately unfriendly welcome with its hint of conflict and intimidation.

There is a suggestion in this scene that things generally are 'twisted', unnatural and unwelcoming, with the possibility of 'grey-backs' infesting the bedding. We anticipate trouble at the deliberate reiteration of the boss's reported annoyance. George needs a welcoming, friendly environment for Lennie's safety so this scene makes the reader apprehensive. Candy has been crippled by an accident; so, too, has Crooks, the stable-buck. This atmosphere of casual violence will be made more dangerous by Lennie's presence.

Nothing is wasted in *Of Mice and Men*; everything matters. An examiner would, however, expect you to recognise that this introduction to the ranch as a world of cripples is a passage of particular significance.

George inspects his bunk

Suspecting that his bed contains vermin, George inspects it cautiously. As he

Violence

does so, Candy chatters on about the boss. We learn that he vents his anger on the black stable-hand, provides the men with whisky and allows a fight between the stable-buck and 'Smitty', one of the skinners. The boss could be worse: Candy insists he's 'a pretty nice fella' and, after all, he keeps the two cripples on the pay-roll. One should not expect urban standards of civilised behaviour on a remote ranch among itinerant labourers, but the atmosphere of latent violence has the potential to create trouble for (and from) Lennie.

The boss arrives

The arrival of the boss justifies our expectations. His black clothes remind the

Authority

reader of the stereotyped 'good' and 'bad' men in westerns. He has a severe 'square steel buckle' on his belt, rather than the more usual ornate one. He is a proud man who wears 'high-heeled boots and spurs' to accentuate his position. He is unsympathetic and authoritarian. His nature is the opposite of Lennie's mild, lumbering, good-heartedness.

Strong as a bull

Again Lennie is described in terms of an animal. This emphasises his great strength. This is further evidence of George's unwitting revealing of the truth of things. Lennie's last name, 'Small', is ironic and amusing.

George supports Lennie

As the boss begins to quiz Lennie, George breaks in loudly to help him. Is

George overprotective, do you think? His constant interruptions serve only to arouse the boss's suspicion. What do you imagine Lennie might have said if he had continued to speak? Later on, Lennie is quite articulate. Perhaps the only real danger here is that Lennie may say something revealing about the incident with the girl in Weed.

George

This incident offers a good example of Steinbeck's narrative skill. The story is revealed a little at a time as reader expectation grows. It takes some forty pages from first mention before the reader gets a complete picture of what happened.

The boss departs

George's comment that Lennie 'Damn near lost us the job' might seem rather harsh. You might think that the opposite is fairer – it was George's long explanations that attracted more intense scrutiny from the boss. Does Lennie provide George with something on which to vent his exasperation when things are not going to plan?

Candy's dog appears

The harmony of nature is contrasted with the aggression and confusion of the bunkhouse by Candy's dog, which is at the end of its useful life, but has provided companionship for its gentle owner for many years. The dog's death foreshadows George's killing of Lennie.

Nature

Curley arrives

Our first impression of Curley is complicated – his 'brown face', 'brown eyes'

and 'tightly curled hair' disguise the menace in his later conduct. His glance is cold and he adopts the stance of a fighter, with his 'hands closed into fists'. Even the way he looks and moves is threatening. His 'work glove' on one hand is intriguing and his high-heeled cowboy boots give him a status above that of the work-hands.

Curley

"Let the big guy talk"

A second confrontation is caused by Lennie's attempts to obey George's instructions to say nothing.

Violence

Curley's presence does not bode well for George and Lennie's safety. This is emphasised by Candy's comments – 'he's alla time picking scraps with big guys'. Since Lennie is a bear-like giant of a man, sooner or later he seems certain to provoke a violent assault from Curley. As Candy goes on to explain, Curley is a small man and therefore he feels that he cannot lose in this kind of situation. This seems very dangerous as Lennie 'don't know no rules' when it comes to fighting.

Curley has a new wife

Curley is proud of his new wife, particularly when she makes others envious

Curley's wife

of him. Notice the implication that his hand is kept soft by the vaseline in his glove in order that he may 'pet' his wife. Steinbeck has already established a frightening connection between Lennie, 'petting', and death, so this is ominous. A confrontation between Lennie and Curley already looks inevitable.

Curley's wife has 'got the eye'

If Curley's wife is not satisfied with their married relationship and is 'eyeing'

Curley

other men, then Curley's self-esteem and confidence will be undermined. He may therefore feel the need to establish his 'manliness' with the workers. If this is true you should notice the way he goes about it. Why does a character like Slim not seem to need to establish his manliness in this way? Curley seems to think that he can gain authority only by physically terrorising others. We later learn that the ranch-hands despise him. Try to decide why the ranch-hands laugh at Curley. Notice that there is an inverse relationship between the size and authority of some characters in the novel.

Candy says Curley's wife has given Slim 'the eye'

Lennie

Candy thinks that Curley's wife is a 'tart'. How vulnerable may Lennie be to such a woman? We have been prepared for this earlier by the references to Lennie and 'girls' and the trouble in Weed. How might Lennie interpret such a woman's behaviour towards him? Is it likely to be the same as the way the other ranch-hands interpret her behaviour?

George is frightened by the situation at the ranch

George is frightened for Lennie's safety, not only because of Curley's aggressiveness, but also because of the way Curley's wife is likely to flaunt her attractiveness. Lennie is frightened of violence, despite his great strength and size, and is not aware of his own physical strength.

Steinbeck subtly introduces another theme of the novel at this point, when George plays a card game of solitaire – loneliness. This connects with the same meaning in the place-name Soledad.

Lennie's frightened appeal to George is quickly followed by a description of the arrival of the grain teams outside. The atmosphere of menace and the fear is emphasised by the harsh and abrasive noises approaching. The success of various films of the novel (notably the Burgess Meredith/Lon Chaney, Jr. classic in 1939) owes something to a narrative style that is reminiscent of theatre and film scripts. Steinbeck himself referred to it as the 'play-novelette' form and wrote that it was 'a tricky little thing designed to teach me to write for the theatre.'

We meet Curley's wife

The extravagance and provocativeness of the girl's dress and make-up make us unsympathetic towards her. Her general appearance seems completely unsuitable for life on a ranch. The dominating colour, red, is also symbolic of a woman with loose morals, as in the expression 'a scarlet woman'. She seems very conscious of herself. But nothing in what you are told directly about her intentions actually suggests that she is being sexually provocative, so why is this impression clearly created? (Steinbeck's use of the word 'bridled' should help you here.) Lennie is clearly impressed by the sensual display of Curley's wife. Various elements of the ranch environment are coming together to form a trap for Lennie. Do you think Lennie could have escaped?

Curley's wife's entry marks out a course that is equally dangerous for herself and for Lennie. It is easy (and, to an extent, right) to condemn her, but remember that we know more of Lennie than she does.

Slim arrives

On learning from Slim that Curley has gone home looking for her, Curley's wife suddenly becomes nervous. There is clearly some sort of tension between them. The suggestion is that her behaviour could be the cause. Try to decide whether she is frightened of Curley. If you think she is, why does she deliberately court disaster? Is she unwittingly provocative and ignorant of the effects of her behaviour?

Slim

Lennie thinks that Curley's wife is pretty

The uncomplicated, bovine Lennie is transfixed by the obvious 'prettiness' of Curley's wife. Whereas the others can see the limitations of her attractions and speculate about her morals, Lennie is conscious only of her animal awareness of the opposite sex. He seems to see her as an animal in heat, or simply as something 'pretty'.

Nature   George senses imminent danger and tries to warn Lennie about the kind of woman Curley's wife is. He calls her 'jail bait' although in fact the consequences of her contact with Lennie will be far worse than any jail sentence.

Lennie tries to free the ear from George's grasp

Lennie intuitively senses trouble and tries to escape. Perhaps he has an animal's gift for sensing danger. George has to balance his instinct to escape against the need to earn money and this need outweighs his misgivings. This decision will cost him dearly in the end.

Slim comes in from the wash room

Slim is a man of 'majesty' and 'authority' and is capable 'of understanding beyond thought'. He is a character of strong moral principles who acts as judge and adviser in the events to come. His is the calm voice of reason.

Slim   Slim's gentle and friendly tone is in marked contrast to the harshness of the rest of the ranch and its brutal inhabitants. Unlike many others in the novel, he is not suspicious of the relationship between George and Lennie and gives them tacit approval. The boss and Curley have reacted aggressively to the pair, but Slim wants them to work on his team. As he is a 'master craftsman', this is a generous gesture. He shows that it is possible to command respect through natural authority rather than through bullying and violence.

Slim is almost the only character who has sufficient confidence in himself to be charitable to others. He is a key figure in understanding the novel and, in particular, in titles like question 1 on page 61.

Carlson arrives

Carlson is at his first appearance a cheerful, good-humoured man who seems to be friendly with Slim. His question about Slim's dog reminds you about George's promise of a pup to Lennie. Notice Steinbeck's impressive economy in the use of dramatic devices to bring the story to its tragic end. See if you can note down how a small number of incidents are enough to make the novel's eventual outcome inevitable.

Carlson says that Candy's dog should be destroyed

Loneliness

Carlson is unsentimental about Candy's dog as he can see no further practical use for it. Although his suggestion is perhaps reasonable, he seems oblivious to the strong bond between Candy and his pet. A parallel is developing between Candy's loneliness and the comfort afforded him by his dog, and the relationship between George and Lennie.

Slim stood up slowly and with dignity

Slim moves with 'dignity' and is concerned for the welfare of George and Lennie. Why does Slim not respond directly to Carlson's suggestion about Candy's dog? His delay adds suspense and therefore tension to the coming discussion with Candy.

Curley comes in spoiling for a fight

Curley

Steinbeck does not allow any sense of security to last for long, and Curley's reappearance interrupts Lennie's delight at the prospect of owning a puppy. His threatening behaviour reminds you that trouble is not far away.

■ Self-test questions Section 2

Uncover the plot

Delete two of the three alternatives given, to find the correct plot. Beware possible misconceptions and muddles.

George and Lennie arrive at the ranch. They are given food/work/bunks by Candy, the boss/swamper/skinner, and signed up by the boss/the boss' son/Curley. The boss is angry that they arrived too late for the day's/weekend's/morning's work, and impressed by/suspicious of/pleased with George's protectiveness of Lennie. Candy/Carlson/Curley, the boss' son, is kind to/indifferent to/antagonistic towards the new men, especially Lennie; they learn from Candy that Curley has recently married a 'tart'/nice girl/prostitute. The whole set-up pleases/scares/interests George, who warns Lennie to have nothing to do with Curley. The other ranch hands return from work. Slim/the stable buck/Whitey is very friendly; Carlson is more concerned with shooting Slim's/Smitty's/Candy's old dog, and asks Slim to give Lennie/George/Candy one of his puppies/rabbits/mice to raise. In the midst of Lennie's excitement at the possibility of owning a pup, Curley returns in search of his itinerant/eminent/errant wife.

Who? What? Why? When? Where? How?

1   Who was Whitey, and – according to Candy – what kind of man was he? Why do you think Candy tells George this?

2   How does George make up his bed, and how does Lennie do his?

3   How many miles does George tell the boss they have walked; how many do you think they really did walk?
4   What is Lennie's surname, and why does Carlson find it funny?
5   What does the boss suspect George of doing, and why?
6   Why is Curley's glove full of Vaseline?
7   When can George and Lennie leave the ranch, according to George? When does Lennie want to leave?
8   What is a jerkline skinner?
9   Why did Slim drown four of his puppies?
10   Why does Carlson really want to shoot Candy's dog?

Who is this?
1   Who has got 'a crooked back where a horse kicked him', and 'reads a lot. Got books in his room'?
2   Who wore 'a soiled brown Stetson hat, and ...high-heeled boots and spurs to prove he was not a labouring man'?
3   Who is 'not much of a talker', but 'strong as a bull'?
4   Who is 'grey of muzzle, and with pale, blind old eyes'?
5   Who 'don't never listen nor... ast no questions'?
6   Whose 'glance was at once calculating and pugnacious'?
7   Who 'ain't givin' nobody a chance', according to Candy?
8   Who is 'purty', with 'the eye'?
9   Who had 'full, rouged lips and wide-spaced eyes, heavily made up'?
10   Whose 'authority was so great that his word was taken on any subject, be it politics or love'?

Who's in charge?
The nature of authority – the different forms it can take, whether or not it is effective, how it is exerted – is an important theme in the novel. With this in mind, answer the following questions.
1   In what order do the three men enter the bunk-house? Is this significant, do you think?
2   According to Candy, how does the stable-buck react to the boss' anger? Do you think that the fact that he reads a lot is important in this respect?
3   What is the boss' attitude to George and Lennie, and now does his dress reflect this?
4   Is George's 'authority' over Lennie portrayed in a completely positive light in this section? Give reasons for your answer.
5   Does Curley have any authority? If so, how does he achieve/exert it?
6   Slim has authority: what makes him different from the boss? How is his manner described?

Sunshine shapes
In this section there are three powerful images evoking the sunshine. Quote the relevant lines. Do you think they are just 'strong descriptions', or have they a deeper significance?

Background noise
Sound/noise is also an important feature of life at the ranch. List five sounds that George and Lennie hear coming from out side the bunk-house. What effect(s) do you think these background noises achieve? Has the author used this technique before?

Section 3

The setting for this section is the interior of the bunkhouse. Candy's dog is shot by Carlson. George and Lennie draw Candy into their dream of a place of their own. Curley picks a fight with Lennie and has his hand crushed.

'Although there was evening brightness showing...'

Nature

This section opens with a description of the surrounding environment. The 'evening brightness', so beautifully described in the first section of the book, is noticeably excluded from this scene, and the atmosphere in the bunkhouse is now that of 'dusk'. This change of mood maintains the sense of foreboding and provides the setting for the next important piece of action.

Slim drowns some of the litter

Slim has agreed to let Lennie have one of the puppies. It is characteristic of

Slim

him that he makes little of the gift. We learn that Slim killed several of the puppies at birth, but this is completely different from the killing by Lennie of his puppy. Slim kills the puppies for a reason, whereas Lennie does not realise what he is doing. Notice how this affects the way the two characters see their own actions.

George describes Lennie's delight when he is given the puppy. The description provides a comic touch with the suggestion that the huge and lumbering Lennie might climb into the box with the pups.

Premonitions

Steinbeck continually provides hints and premonitions of disaster. Hardly a

Lennie

page goes by without some reference to Lennie's tendency to get into trouble. George observes that Lennie is sure to get into trouble sooner or later – 'like you always done before'. Curley carries a constant threat of violence and his wife is 'jail bait'. Disaster seems to be imminent and hangs, sword-like, over George and Lennie.

The emphasis on Lennie's strength not only demonstrates Slim's generosity in praising him but also serves to prepare us for the outcome of the violence which occurs later when Curley attacks Lennie.

George confides in Slim

Having created the sympathetic character of Slim, Steinbeck uses the dramatic device of a conversation to reveal more about the relationship of George and Lennie before the story moves on. George reveals the circumstances which brought about their unlikely partnership. We learn about their origins in

Auburn, Lennie's Aunt Clara and their mutual need for companionship. More is also revealed about the absolute trust Lennie puts in George, together with his sometimes frighteningly unquestioning obedience.

The story of Lennie and the Sacramento River is important for illustrating various aspects of their friendship. It shows how fully Lennie trusts George and how forgiving he is, but what do you think it reveals about George's attitude to Lennie? Does it give any hint of why George remains loyal to Lennie?

Understanding and interpretation of the George/Lennie relationship is, of course, central to many essays on the novel. Note that it is not static: various past events are recalled. Apart from the Sacramento River, remember Weed, Aunt Clara, etc.

The isolation and loneliness of the ranch-hand's life

Slim's readiness to praise Lennie shows not only his thoughtfulness but also the generosity in his character. He sees Lennie's true worth. Slim's assessment of situations is treated like the word of God. No doubt George is proud that Lennie's true worth is appreciated by Slim. Slim also says that there is plenty of violence in the environment of the ranch and that 'meanness' is bred by isolation. We learn that George has no relations and

Slim

has been saved from loneliness and perhaps from disillusionment by Lennie. Loneliness and isolation become a preoccupying theme of the novel from this point onwards, highlighting the plight of the itinerant worker who goes through life without putting down roots. How far do you think this explains the reason for George and Lennie's partnership?

You learn more about the girl in the red dress

The seriousness of the incident in Weed is underlined by the revelation that Lennie would have been 'lynched' (hanged) had they caught him.

The colour of the girl's dress in Weed — red — is also ominously the dominant colour in the description of Curley's wife.

Violence

Slim carefully considers the evidence which George gives him about Lennie. He believes George's assertion that Lennie is not dangerous and had not intended to harm the girl in Weed. However, you should notice the escalation of violence in Lennie's behaviour as described by George and the fact that Lennie was fascinated by the blatant sexuality of Curley's wife. Whether Lennie's state of innocence will survive, given this kind of provocation, might be hard to predict and you need to try to answer for yourself the question of why Lennie needs to 'pet' things.

Lennie takes the puppy to bed – but is caught

The limits of Lennie's understanding are displayed when he puts the life of

the puppy at risk by removing it so soon from its mother. It shows just how powerful is his urge for 'petting' and how much it seems to dominate his personality.

Notice Slim's appraisal of the situation. Does he perhaps seriously underestimate the harm which might befall Lennie as a result of his needs and his immense strength?

Lennie

Carlson returns

Candy and his dog have been together for so long that Candy is not aware of the dog's offensive smell. Carlson says 'he ain't no good to himself' by way of justification for killing the dog. Notice also that the way Carlson talks about Candy's dog echoes the way the stable buck, Crooks, says the ranch-hands behave towards him.

In describing precisely how he will shoot the dog painlessly, even down

to the exact location for the bullet, Carlson may unwittingly be showing George how he will eventually dispose of Lennie 'humanely'. See if you feel that Carlson's detachment and cool analysis of the situation is harsh, or justified. Lennie is eventually shot by the same gun, and in the same place in the back of the head, as Candy's dog. These 'echoing' devices in the book give it a strong sense of unity.

Violence

"Well, you ain't bein' kind to him..."

With these words Carlson is ironically 'sentencing' Lennie, who will later suffer the same fate as the dog. Carlson assumes that Candy can soon get another pet – just as at the end of the novel he seems to assume that George can easily get another friend. Carlson, like some of the other characters, does not appreciate these bonds.

Candy and his dog are an obvious parallel to George and Lennie, even to

the way the dog follows Candy around in the same way Lennie follows George. Just as Candy feels tied down by his relationship with his dog, so George feels trapped by his sense of responsibility for Lennie. This may be a clue to the real reason for the loneliness of the ranch-hands: they shy away from committing themselves to relationships and responsibility.

Loneliness

You may regard *Of Mice and Men* as a realistic novel, but you need to be aware of the force of symbolism. One of the most important links between Lennie and the animal kingdom is that to Candy's old helpless dog who must be destroyed.

Slim passes judgement on the dog

Slim

Slim's opinions are valued by all the ranchers and his pronouncement about Candy's dog seals its fate. By appealing to others to do the same for him if he should ever 'get old and a cripple', Slim paves the way for the killing of Lennie, who is mentally 'crippled'. Slim's considered verdict has the force of law on the ranch.

Whit

The character of Whit remains undeveloped. The episode which shows him excited by an item in a magazine slows down the pace of the action and contributes to the suspense generated by the proposal to shoot the dog. It also serves to illustrate the poverty of experience and education in most of the ranch-hands.

Carlson has got a Luger and is told to take a shovel

Carlson is not a cowboy, but does possess a hand-gun — not the traditional

Violence

Colt but a German pistol. The conversation about the gun lets George know where it is kept. It is the sensitive Slim who points out that Carlson will need a shovel in order to give the dog a decent burial. Compare the shooting of the dog with the shooting of Lennie. Steinbeck emphasises the long wait by mentioning muted sounds, like 'shuffle', 'rippled', and 'gnawing', which contrast with the eventual 'shot'.

The stable-buck arrives

Immediately after the dog's death we are reminded of Lennie and his obsessions, when the stable-buck comes to say that Lennie is 'messin' around' with Slim's pups. George's words a few lines further on — "If that crazy bastard's foolin' around…" – ring with double meaning, for the words 'foolin' around' are usually applied in America to intimate behaviour between males and females. Later on it will be Curley's wife – and her seeming desire to 'fool around' with the ranch-hands – who preoccupies George.

Curley's wife is 'a looloo'

Whit uses the name of Candy's dog – Lulu – to describe Curley's wife. His

Curley's wife

description of her 'concealing nothing' and giving everyone the 'eye', coming straight after the description of Lennie's behaviour with the dogs in the barn, emphasises Lennie's innate ability to get into trouble. It is unfortunate that George and Lennie's have arrived at a moment when trouble seems likely to erupt. Steinbeck builds the tension and expectation towards a climax which will fuse together all these different elements.

You should consider the fix that George finds himself in. He says of Curley's wife, 'She's gonna make a mess' – so why doesn't he move out at once to avoid trouble? Whit underlines the basic predicament of itinerant workers; their existence is mean and centres around violence, cheap sex, drinking and fighting. They earn insufficient money to be able to save up and build a 'stake' for a more deeply satisfying life. Why is it that they always spend their money on 'blackjack' and 'whores', as Crooks observes? Consider the extent to which their desire for carefree enjoyment and pleasure is the 'serpent' in their Garden of Eden.

The importance of the cleaning of the gun

Carlson may be practical and have the cold nerve necessary to kill the dog, but he is fairly callous too. He makes no effort to conceal the cleaning of the recently fired gun from Candy, who must find the sound of the snapping of the ejector a painful reminder of his dog's death.

The killing of Candy's dog: a scene from a play?

The killing of Candy's dog is an interesting example of the technique which Steinbeck is trying out in this book, which is a cross between a novel and a play or drama. Each of the six sections (actually split into chapters in some editions) deals with one scene. Each opens with a description of the scene and is followed by dialogue between characters who enter and exit in the same way that they would in a play or film. If you look carefully you will notice that almost every piece of description or storytelling is like a stage direction to a theatre or film director. Each section (or chapter) could easily be translated into an act or scene on stage and, indeed, when the book was first performed as a play (in November 1937) in Steinbeck's own adaptation, the dialogue was changed very little. Another thing which should remind you of a playscript is that very few characters are used – far fewer than in most novels. The length is also significant, the stage version running for some two hours. It is hardly necessary to make any cuts at all, which is probably unique in novel adaptations for the stage.

How effective is Steinbeck's play/novel technique, do you think? Why do you think he experimented with this way of writing? In order to help you answer these important questions, think about how effective this method is in getting the reader to imagine the events and the conversations which take place, and how easy it is to follow what is going on. Consider whether this technique works better than in the traditionally written novel.

Another thing to consider is that many novels which are now highly regarded were written before the widespread availability of films and television – or even before their invention. You may already have read some such works, probably with great enjoyment. But the invention of film and television sometimes changed the way drama was made to work. You can always re-read interesting parts of a book, but it is more difficult to look back over parts of a cinema or live theatre production. Steinbeck may therefore have written *Of Mice And Men* in the way he did because of changes in the nature of the media which were available. Remember that the book was written in 1937.

Curley arrives, looking for his wife, as usual

Slim

Curley is clearly looking for a victim on whom he can vent his frustration and anger. This is especially dangerous because he has been a boxer of some ability. Curley demands to know where Slim is. Presumably he suspects him to be a rival for the affections of his wife. Slim is a mysterious and potentially dangerous character. He has a genuinely caring nature and his reason for going out to the barn is typical of him – he makes a special point of dealing with the mule's injury himself. But he has a strong 'presence' whenever he appears, and is a powerful figure of authority.

As a typical ranch-hand, Whit is eager to witness or participate in any brawling. He too encourages George to go out to witness the possible confrontation.

George tries to stay out of trouble

Dreams

George wants to stay out of trouble and avoid getting the sack. The choice between leaving the ranch or staying to earn a 'stake' becomes increasingly vital. George is torn between the need to protect Lennie and the fulfilment of his dream of a homestead. He wants more from life than the Whits and Carlsons of the ranch-world – he has clear and definite ambitions.

George's view of women

George

George seems to have a very biased and basic view of women and sees them only as instruments to relieve certain physical urges, as a device to 'get ever'thing outa his system all at once, an' no messes'. He does not express the need for any female companionship beyond this and his lack of trust is further illustrated by the fact that women do not feature in his dream of a smallholding. This may indicate that, in spite of his relationship with Lennie, George fears a deep and loving relationship.

Is the farm just a dream?

George talks wistfully about his mental picture of the farm. He sits 'entranced with his own picture'. George's dream-like description slows down the pace of the novel at this point and provides a period of 'pastoral' calm before the storm. The life and surroundings which George imagines are the very opposite

of his present existence, always on the move as he is between one farm and the next for seasonal work. His life, and Lennie's, would be more closely related to nature on his dream farm – as he says, 'when we put in a crop, why we'd be there to take the crop up', so the cycle of the natural rhythms of nature

Dreams would be complete. The situation sounds so much like a dream that it comes as something of a surprise to the reader to learn that the place does in fact exist, and is not just a bedtime story thought up to amuse Lennie. This makes his need for a 'stake' more easy to understand.

Of Mice and Men requires subtly detailed reading. It is, for instance, easy to condemn the idea of the farm as just a dream. In fact it is attainable, making its loss more poignant, but also providing an element of hope (see question 1, page 61).

Plans and dreams: why *Of Mice and Men*?

Man's longing for a piece of land was a favourite theme of Steinbeck's and he returned to it in nearly every novel he wrote. Although you can see several particular examples of personal tragedy in *Of Mice And Men*, Steinbeck clearly also means the story to be a parable of the human condition – as the novel's final title indicates. In the poem from which the title is taken, Burns wrote that 'the best laid schemes o' mice an' men gang aft a-gley'. The phrase 'gang aft a-gley' literally means 'go often astray', but Steinbeck does not translate Burns' 'aft' as 'often', but instead as 'always'. Notice how in *Of Mice And Men* Crooks says: 'Nobody never gets to heaven, and nobody gets no land.' *Of Mice and Men* is a highly appropriate title for the novel. All the plans go astray: not just George and Lennie's, but those of Curley, his wife, Crooks and Candy. What other reason can you think of for the choice of title?

Or is the farm really possible?

George suddenly realises that what has been until this point only a distant

dream is now a real possibility, with Candy's involvement and contribution. It offers them all the prospect of self-respect and companionship. The characters have a moment of hope before being plunged straight into conflict. The ranch-hands' shared sense of euphoria and of the beauty of the dream is in stark

Dreams contrast to the surroundings in which they actually find themselves.

Slim and Curley return from the barn

Curley's suspicions have proved to be groundless and he is trying to apologise. This seems likely only to increase his humiliation and his feelings of frustration and anger.

Candy says he should have shot the dog himself

Candy seems to feel that he has shown a lack of courage in not shooting his dog himself and with this admission the dream of the men is broken. At the end of the novel George must take the initiative to save Lennie from Curley, who would kill him in a painful, long, drawn-out way.

Curley's temper rises

Carlson remarks that Curley should make his wife stay home, if he doesn't

Curley

like her wandering round the ranch. This serves to aggravate Curley's rising temper, with devastating consequences. The way Curley moves from man to man, getting insults and jokes thrown at him, indicates that Carlson's assessment of his character is probably correct. He does seem to be a coward, despite his notoriously violent streak. Carlson seems to enjoy deliberately making the situation with Curley worse because he is confident of his own ability to handle any resulting violence. Candy also enjoys joining in the attack on Curley. Although he is only one-handed – and therefore in no position to defend himself physically – he is in the company of George, Slim and Carlson, and so is safe from attack. Unfortunately, this leaves Lennie exposed as a target.

Curley turns his anger onto Lennie

It is typical of Curley that he should pick on Lennie for his display of violence.

Violence

In picking on the large but apparently harmless man, Curley demonstrates his own cowardice. There is an irony in the fact that it is Lennie's happy thoughts about the farm that leave a smile on his face, which is misinterpreted by Curley. Despite his size, Lennie has two distinct disadvantages; he will not act unless commanded to by George, and he is terrified by aggression. Because of this he does not make any attempt to defend himself. Curley is a vicious fighter and is out to inflict grave damage on Lennie, who needs George to 'trigger' his reaction. Notice the use of animal imagery here: Lennie stands like a 'bear' with 'paws' covering his face, but Curley is 'the dirty little rat'.

Are you able to predict Lennie's response? His immense strength and tenacious grip crush Curley's hand. This is not aggression but more of a reflex action; it is a defensive move similar to that of a bear, which responds to aggression by hugging – a sort of deadly embrace.

Suddenly Lennie lets go

This shows the extent of the responsibility that George carries for Lennie's actions. Lennie is almost uncontrollable and it takes a great deal of effort on George's part to penetrate Lennie's fear and first get him to defend himself and then to release his grip on Curley's hand.

> In understanding and writing about this book, it is always necessary to look beyond the event to hints of future consequences. We may not be concerned at Curley's fate, but this scene is dangerous in revealing the limits of George's responsibility for Lennie.

Hands

As you read the book you may be struck by the number of times Steinbeck refers, in one way or another, to hands. In fact the word is used well over one hundred times and this frequency is perhaps a little puzzling; Steinbeck sometimes seems to go out of his way to use the word unnecessarily. On one level its frequent use is fairly clear and straightforward, as when Lennie's hands are called 'paws'; Candy has one hand missing; Curley keeps one hand in a glove full of vaseline; the colour of Crook's palms are noted (they are pink); George has 'small, strong hands'; Slim's hands are 'delicate in their action as those of a temple dancer'; and Curley's wife has hands which are described only in terms of fingers and red fingernails.

But sometimes a character's hands seem to have a life of their own, as when Lennie's 'hands went into the pocket again' and when his 'closed hand slowly obeyed'. Later on George 'looked at his right hand that had thrown the gun away' and Slim 'subdued one hand with the other and held it down'. Contrary to what you might expect, however, the use of the word 'hand' to describe a common agricultural worker is extremely rare in the book.

How far do you think that Steinbeck is deliberately dehumanising individuals into physical parts, rather than showing them as whole people? Is he suggesting that the characters are lonely, incomplete people in search of a way to become whole?

Slim takes charge of the situation

Slim's surprise and horror give greater emphasis to Lennie's strength and the

damage of which he is capable. Although Curley's attack has resulted in him getting what he deserves, Slim still has enough compassion to take care of the injured man and, despite the fact that he too has suffered abuse from Curley before the fight, he has the natural authority to take responsibility for getting him to a doctor.

Slim

Slim is definitely master of the situation and has the shrewdness to manipulate the situation to George's and Lennie's advantage. He turns Curley's pride against him, and suggests that if the truth about the fight were to become known, Curley would become a laughing-stock.

George's worst fears are beginning to come true; in his single-minded pursuit of a 'stake', and in his deliberate disregard for the danger of their situation, and its probable consequences for Lennie, he is risking a dreadful calamity.

George says he warned people to beware of Lennie

Lennie

George knows that in any situation that causes Lennie to panic, he will hang on like a bear. The fight is only one aspect of the possible problems on the ranch, but it causes us to wonder what will happen if the same reaction in Lennie is triggered off by Curley's wife.

Lennie cannot tell the difference between right and wrong – he has only an animal's sense of self-protection. The prospect of 'tending the rabbits' gives us some idea of what is important in Lennie's life, as does his passionate care for them even when they exist only in his imagination. But although Lennie becomes roused by any threat to his imaginary rabbits, this is not because he has strong moral views about right and wrong. Lennie is a confusingly amoral character – he has only intuition to guide him.

Section 4

This section is set in the harness room of the barn. The dreams of the men for a place of their own are interrupted by the 'catalyst' of Curley's wife. She destroys their budding friendships and poisons the dream.

Section 4 opens with a carefully detailed description of the harness room of the stables. It would be easy to construct and decorate a stage set from the detailed instructions given. This description is probably derived from Steinbeck's own experience. The neat, workman-like impression which Steinbeck creates indicates that Crooks, who lives in the room, has a committed and professional attitude towards his charges, the horses.

Crooks

Crooks

Crooks, as his name suggests, is 'crooked' in the spine as a result of an accident. He is not an itinerant worker like the others and this room represents 'home'. Crooks is supposed to be exceptional in that he is literate and conscious of his rights – 'large gold-rimmed spectacles' are prominent above his bed and he has 'a mauled copy of the California civil code for 1905'. These are symbols of his learning. Crooks is 'proud and aloof' and he has a strength of character which demands respect. His eyes 'glitter with intensity', and his 'deep black wrinkles' and 'pain-tightened lips' emphasise his experience of silent suffering. He is in constant pain and treats himself as he does the horses, with liniment. This is the private act of a private man – he is therefore understandably annoyed at the interruption from Lennie.

Most of the characters in *Of Mice and Men* have significance beyond their often brief appearances. Certainly this is true of Crooks whom you can cite in many essays dealing with subjects such as victims, prejudice, solitude, independence, etc.

Crooks is a solitary man

The character of Crooks is drawn by Steinbeck with considerable sympathy. Crooks is a solitary man and does not welcome intrusions into his privacy: his 'scowl' when Lennie arrives can be attributed to this. Much of Crooks' pride and truculence is a defence against the racial prejudice he experiences from the other work-hands. He has been excluded by the inhabitants of the bunkhouse because of his colour. He says 'they say I stink', which reminds us of Carlson's remark about Candy's dog. From what he reveals about this treatment, it would seem that his attitude is justified and that he has little reason at first to trust Lennie.

Lennie has been left on his own

You might think it very foolhardy of George not to stay behind to keep an

Dreams

eye on Lennie. But for Steinbeck, it may have been essential for the development of the story to get rid of most of the hands, in order to allow the physical cripples (Crooks and Candy) and the mental cripple (Lennie) to get together without fear of interruption. Consider what you learn about each man as a result of their conversations here and what you learn about the dreams and aspirations of the itinerant workers of the time. Ignore, for a moment, their particular circumstances, and you may conclude that their hopes and dreams are not peculiar just to their time and country, but are common to most people.

"Why ain't you wanted?" Lennie asked

Lennie's attitude gives Crooks little reason to feel antagonised. His usual

Crooks

defence against the white ranch-hands is to remain 'aloof', but he seems to recognise in Lennie a genuine, uncomplicated and open nature that offers friendship without any hidden conditions or threats. Look at the circumstances under which Lennie later becomes threatening and try to decide whether you think he is an unpredictable person.

Candy is in the bunkhouse

Candy has remained behind at the ranch, excited by the prospects that the new farm has suddenly opened up for him. He sees the farm as an escape. George has suggested that Candy should take care of Lennie on the farm, and he takes this offer very seriously. This will also help Candy cope with the loss of his dog, and subtly reinforces the idea of Lennie as a large and gentle (but potentially dangerous) animal which needs supervision and care.

Authority

Lennie tells Crooks about the dream farm

Lennie seems quite articulate about the prospect of living 'on the fatta the lan', although you know that he is only repeating what has often been said to him. Nonetheless, you may be surprised by the way Lennie is able to express himself. The idea of the farm begins to attract Crooks and he invites Lennie to sit down. The fact that Lennie is disobeying George's instructions to keep the farm a secret gives this episode extra tension.

Crooks is by nature proud and reserved, but he is also lonely and he decides that he can tell Lennie secrets by way of their conversation which will not then be revealed or turned against him later in ridicule. Crooks is another character, like Candy, whose life is isolated and unsatisfying. We learn that he is not a typical black man of that time with roots in slavery, but has enjoyed a comparatively high status and standard of living.

Loneliness

Blacks are rare in California and in this area of Soledad, so his family have been the victims of prejudice. The isolation which this produced was made worse by the disapproval of Crooks' father for his white friends. Colour prejudice makes Crooks' position on the ranch lonely and isolated.

Does Lennie ever understand what goes on around him?

Crooks is correct in his assessment of Lennie; he has not really taken in the revelations about Crooks' background. Lennie lives in a state of innocence, and the many injustices of the world are outside his understanding. Crooks lowers his guard and shows us, through what he tells Lennie, that he suffers intense loneliness. He suggests that George and Lennie are partners because of the 'unspoken' companionship of simply staying with each other. He sees his own black skin and his deformity as a double disadvantage.

Crooks seems unable to resist a rare opportunity to inflict pain on another person – he is usually the victim. Crooks' suggestion to Lennie is vindictive and heartless. Notice how his 'face lighted with pleasure in his torture' of Lennie. Crooks unwittingly predicts how Lennie will be treated in the future – like a wild animal, not tied up, but shot like Candy's dog.

Violence

Supposing George gets hurt and doesn't come back?

With George away, Lennie has no defence against this attack. Crooks is playing a dangerous game in attempting to test their relationship. Lennie is alarmed by what Crooks says: 'Suddenly Lennie's eyes centred and grew quiet'. This incident shows you that, under certain circumstances, Lennie can be roused and, when he is, he is ready to act. We get a better idea of the sheer size of George's responsibility and of Lennie's helplessness.

Loneliness

Crooks' quiet 'Maybe you can see now...' reveals the pathos of his loneliness and isolation. Crooks craves companionship because he knows that human contact acts as a confirmation of what a person thinks and believes. Without regular contact with other people, Crooks feels that 'he got nothing to measure by'.

George ain't hurt

Nature

Bear imagery is again used to describe Lennie. There is also a hint of a circus performance in the way he growls his way back to the barrel. Notice another parallel – when George first got to know Lennie he used to 'have a hell of a lot of fun with 'im', which is not unlike what Crooks does here.

Crooks understands why people search for happiness

Crooks is rather scornful of the dream as Lennie explains it to him – 'You're

Dreams

nuts', he says. In some ways Crooks has put his enforced isolation to good use, and what he says contains some useful thoughts about life in general. Crooks compares human hopes with religious belief and says that the search for 'a little piece of land' is like the search for heaven. He has a fairly cynical view of both. However, his experiences and comments create tension and anxiety, because George, Lennie and Candy seem to be so near to realising their dream.

Candy arrives

Crooks is disappointed when his new friendship with Lennie is threatened by

Loneliness

the intrusion of someone else. But he is at the same time pleased and excited at the unusual prospect of company and a friendly evening. Notice how Lennie innocently disregards the fact that this is Crooks' private room, while Candy is acutely aware of the social distance between himself and Crooks. But the room represents Crooks' enforced isolation. Equally, Candy has just gone through the experience of losing his dog, and so he too has had a kind of enforced loneliness thrust upon him.

With Candy the age-old prejudices of race have prevented him from ever getting to know Crooks, and it takes the innocent actions of Lennie to bring the two men together. Part of Lennie's function in the book is to act as a catalyst in the relationships between other characters. Notice how at first the conversation hovers around safe topics, such as their common admiration for Slim. Slim has been in Crooks' room before. Like the boss, with whom he is here mentioned, Slim's natural authority gives him the right.

The farm

Conversation soon turns to the topic of the farm. In spite of his desperate need to accumulate money quickly, George has gone 'out on the town' with the others. He intends only to sit and drink. Crooks' reflections about the way the itinerant workers never end up with anything seems to contain a considerable amount of truth.

Candy's outburst here: 'Sure they all want it', contains an idea that is central to the whole book. Owning their own land, with the opportunity to see the seasons through the whole year, would give status and self-esteem to the low-paid workers. It would give them encouragement and pride, with incentive and satisfaction in life.

 A series of excellent quotations to sum up the dream of land: 'I planted crops for damn near ever'body in this state, but they weren't my crops...' (Candy), 'I seen guys nearly crazy with loneliness for land...' (Crooks) and many others.

Dreams

Crooks thinks the chances of their successfully achieving their 'dream farm' are remote. Few have achieved it before – none in Crooks' experience – yet they do seem so near, with only one month's further savings necessary. This closeness to achieving their goal contributes to the novel's final sense of tragedy. As so often in tragedy, the central character, Lennie, dies as a result of the 'fatal flaw' in his personality. In this case it is a striving for affection, shown in his need for 'petting'. The book is also a tragedy in the sense that the lives and fates of the main characters are not rooted in an ordered society: they live instead in a world where normal social order and normal human relationships are not available to them. Their lives are usually directionless and chaotic as a result.

As in most of Steinbeck's novels, the main image of the book is a kind of earthly paradise or 'heaven' which, for Americans, usually meant a network of small farms, worked by their owners for their own benefit. It is a vision of prosperity and harmony which embraces good fellowship and the independence of the individual. But in Steinbeck's novels, as Crooks puts it: 'Nobody never gets to heaven'.

Crooks is drawn into the dream

Crooks

Despite his cynicism, Crooks is drawn into the same dream of a better life and of companionship. During this brief episode, he has moved from sullen resentment at the intrusion of others to companionable excitement. The proud isolation and prickliness we saw earlier are clearly a protective façade to conceal his frustration and loneliness.

Curley's wife appears

The description of Curley's wife emphasises her sensuousness. Isolated on the

Curley's wife

ranch, she too is lonely and looking for company. Curley has abandoned his wife for a visit to a brothel. Does he prefer the company of prostitutes to her? If so, it explains the viciousness of her attacks on those others who have been left behind. Is she, like them, some sort of 'weak one'? Is her insult a challenge to them to act 'strongly'? Certainly Curley's neglect

of her is characteristic of him, and indicates that there is a very poor basis for their marriage. Curley's wife is not looking for her husband this time but for male company – either to satisfy her sexual needs, or to get back at Curley. Is she sure herself why she behaves the way she does?

Lennie watches Curley's wife and is fascinated

Loneliness

Notice how Lennie responds to her obvious sexuality whenever she appears. Throughout this episode, Lennie remains transfixed by her.

Curley's wife is dangerous because going with her can result in a man being beaten up by her husband. What she claims, though, about the men being 'scared of each other',

seems to point to another aspect of their loneliness – that the men make a conscious choice to remain solitary. The casual nature of their relationships and their restless drifting mean that none of them is able to build up trust in another.

"Jus' the ol' one-two..."

Curley's wife flares up and tells them how Curley spends all his time in the

Curley

house talking about what he is going to do to "guys he don't like, and he don't like nobody". This reinforces what we already know about Curley; his size seems to make him feel that he has to prove himself. He seems obsessed by a need to establish his supremacy over others (like an animal) and, presumably, his 'ownership' of his wife is another facet of this.

Perhaps this is why Curley went into town without his wife – he seems to regard her as more of a possession than a loving partner. She is yet another character who craves companionship but in her case, her sex, and Curley are obstacles to her search for friendship. She seems to need to captivate men, as if she needs reassurance of the effect she has on them.

Loneliness

Curley's wife mirrors the ranch-hands in her loneliness and in her dream of a better life. She is evidently of limited intelligence. Apart from her unsatisfactory marriage to the boss' son, her claim to superiority comes from the fact that 'a guy tol' me he could put me in pitchers': already, in the 1930s, a cliché and a chat-up line to deceive the gullible. She is abusive towards the men – perhaps because she secretly feels that she is too much like them – and seems to need to dominate them. You might conclude that in some ways Curley and his wife are two of a kind.

Curley's wife turns her attention to Lennie

Curley's wife's long look at Lennie causes him 'embarrassment'. The way she

Curley's wife

talks to Lennie has sexual undertones. She is attracted by someone who can beat Curley. Why do you think this is? Lennie does not understand the double meaning in Curley's wife's words, but Crooks does and he tries to protect Lennie. Perhaps Crooks has derived some new strength from his contact with Lennie and Candy, because you have not seen him assert himself in this way before. But by attempting to confront Curley's wife – a white woman – he is putting himself at great risk.

Racial prejudice is not in the forefront of the book, but is a key part of the theme of exploitation of the weak, of creating a society of victims. Curley's wife's threats to Crooks form a particularly unpleasant example of racial prejudice.

Crooks is humiliated by Curley's wife

Crooks has gained confidence by the open nature of Lennie and the

Crooks

friendliness of Candy. Steinbeck is pointing out how people become stronger through the support and companionship of others. All this is taken away by what Curley's wife says. She re-establishes the brutal power of white over black, typically by sexual innuendo and manipulation. Her threat of 'framing' Crooks, alleging sexual interference, would certainly be sufficient to get him hanged. This episode prepares you for the immediate rough-justice of the lynch-mob that pursues Lennie at the end of the novel.

Throughout this section Lennie has revealed surprising skill as a conversationalist. He has also shown a growing sense of confidence, as Crooks and Candy and he all share their dreams. But the outburst from Curley's wife reduces him to the state of a helpless child. Notice how Steinbeck uses the word 'whined' to underline the animal imagery.

The reappearance of the old prejudices makes Crooks withdraw into himself again. His response to oppression is to return to the way he was: he 'had reduced himself to nothing'. In fact it is Curley's wife who has done this to him. This is, of course, also what many of the characters in the novel have done – or are doing – to themselves.

Curley's wife

Curley's wife shows appalling viciousness, and by humiliating first Crooks and Candy, then Lennie, she is setting the scene for the final destruction of Lennie. Her inviting attitude towards Lennie, together with the suggestion of more to follow, creates a growing sense of danger.

George returns

On his return George shows annoyance at Lennie being in Crooks' room. He is also cross at Candy because he wanted to keep the farm a secret, mainly because of his fear that, if the boss were to hear that they planned to quit as soon as they had enough money, he might fire them at once.

Crooks returns to rubbing his back with liniment. This takes us back to the opening of the scene and is another example of Steinbeck's frequent use of dramatic 'echoes', and repeated patterns and cycles in the book. For Crooks, nothing has changed.

Section 5

This section begins in the great barn, where Lennie has just accidentally killed his puppy. Curley's wife confides in Lennie, rather as Crooks did. This results in her death and the start of the man-hunt for Lennie.

This section again starts with evocative scene-setting. Notice how Steinbeck

Nature

appeals to the reader's sense of hearing as well as sight. The visual detail is supported by the onomatopoeia of 'nibble', 'wisp', 'stamped', 'bit', 'rattled', 'buzz' and 'humming'. (Onomatopoeia is the use of words which sound like the action or idea being described). It all creates a warm and lazy atmosphere.

Lennie is in the barn

Lennie

Noises made by the men outside – 'clang', 'shouts', 'jeering' – intrude on the quiet atmosphere. The barn is a fitting environment for the gentle and uncomplicated nature of Lennie. See if you can think of any special significance in Steinbeck's choice of such a setting.

The puppy is dead

Lennie has killed the puppy by clumsily petting it. His tendency to inflict

Lennie

damage through trying to show love is becoming more pronounced. There is a moment of great pathos when he 'unburies' the puppy. He is struggling to come to terms with what he has done and particularly with his disobedience. The inner turmoil that this misfortune has caused to Lennie prepares him for the coming scene with Curley's wife.

Curley's wife is attracted to Lennie because he has got the better of her husband. She has worked out a complicated arrangement to ensure that she can safely be alone with Lennie in the barn without interruption. But Lennie is acutely aware of the consequences of any possible further disobedience and tries hard not to disobey George's instructions.

Curley's wife appears

Steinbeck has created a 'tragic' and doom-laden atmosphere in which we are

Curley's wife

very aware of Lennie's instability. Appropriately, given the way Curley's wife's part in the novel is about to come to an end, she wears a 'bright cotton dress' and 'red ostrich feathers'. You know already how strongly Lennie is attracted to the colour red. Her face is 'made up' and her 'curls' are in place. She has obviously made herself as seductive as possible.

'Then all of Lennie's woe came back on him.'

Dreams

Lennie is particularly vulnerable here because of his unhappiness. He is mourning the death of the puppy and is terrified that it may have robbed him of any chance of the 'dream farm'. This makes him receptive to the offer of companionship and consolation, in spite of George's previous warnings to stay away from Curley's wife and not to talk to her.

The description of the death of the puppy foreshadows what is about to happen to Curley's wife. This incident tells us more about the character of Curley's wife – we see her vulnerable side and her humanity in consoling Lennie – but it also gives the scene tension and a high potential for danger.

Curley's wife wants to know what is the matter with her

Curley keeps his wife on a tight rein. When she does get the chance to talk

Curley's wife

to someone, the words pour out of her in a 'passion of communication'. In what almost amounts to a soliloquy (because Lennie really isn't paying any attention to most of what she says), Curley's wife reveals her own dreams of a better life. Notice how her dream parallels that of Candy, Crooks and George. Steinbeck has used this technique

Dreams

of 'almost-soliloquy' before, with other characters who share the dream (think back to the conversation Crooks had with Lennie in the harness room). Curley's wife seems to be star-struck and to have taken seriously the flattering promises made by men trying to ingratiate themselves with her. Despite her attempts at sophistication, she seems pathetically naive, notably when she is convinced that her 'ol' lady' stole the letter from Hollywood. Although she mocks the men's dream, underneath she is no different from them. Think again about George's judgement of her as 'jail bait'. Was he fair, do you think?

Curley's wife tells Lennie how she came to marry Curley

Curley met his wife at a dance hall, one evening when she had decided that she could not to stay at home any longer. She does not have the intelligence (or the desire?) to grasp the hollowness of the promises which men make her or to realise they have no intention of ever writing to her 'from Hollywood'. Curley's offer was therefore her last chance of escape. However, she 'don' *like* Curley'.

Of Mice and Men is based on sympathy for the victims of society (see question 3, page 63). This scene places Curley's wife firmly in that group, ironically gaining confidence to tell her story from the presence of the arch-victim himself, Lennie.

As was the case with Crooks, Lennie's innocent and open manner inspires confidence in her. Think about which other character has a way which invites people to confide in him, and see if you can think of any similarities between this other character and Lennie.

Curley's wife finds her 'dream' in the glittery world of show-business, the

Dreams

cinema and glossy magazines. This is in sharp contrast to that of the three men. Her interest in the world of cinema and film stars suggest that her behaviour and clothes are designed to provoke interest and attention rather than to invite intimacy. Despite her sensuality and provocative appearance, she seems only to want to talk to Lennie.

Lennie explains why he likes to pet things

Lennie has moved from mice to the puppy and thence to dreams of owning rabbits. Lennie explains that what attracted him to the rabbits he saw at a fair was their long hair. This helps the transition from rabbits to Curley's wife.

Lennie

To begin with, Curley's wife had been content to snuggle up to Lennie, but now she begins to be alarmed by his obsession with petting. Yet she still does not seem to grasp the danger in Lennie's behaviour and her own closeness to him. She describes him as a big baby, but this underestimates the interest and fascination she has aroused in him.

'Curley's wife laughed at him.'

This is a difficult moment in the book to understand. How deliberate do you

Curley's wife

think is Curley's wife's suggestion that Lennie might fondle her hair? She could be innocently referring to its texture, or knowingly leading Lennie towards a sexual encounter. Her intentions at this moment are crucial in allocating blame for what happens next, but they remain unknown. We cannot be certain whether she was in the barn just to talk companionably

to Lennie, or whether she was intent upon seduction.

Lennie strokes the hair of Curley's wife

In stroking the hair of Curley's wife, Lennie may remind you of how Curley kept his left hand soft for her. Petting seems to Curley to have been at the centre of his marriage, but is uncontrollable in Lennie. Notice how Curley's wife only struggles when her appearance is 'mussed up', which is consistent with her vanity and her self-image.

Lennie panics

Lennie

Lennie's panic gives rise to the use of physical force and the results, as with the puppy, are fatal. It is important to notice that the reason for Lennie's panic and anger is his fear that George may discover that Lennie has broken his promise to him. George uses the threat of the loss of the 'dream farm' and the rabbits to keep Lennie under control.

In your work on *Of Mice and Men* you need to be aware of Steinbeck's subtle choice of words: his diction. Writing on the death of Curley's wife, you should note the frequency of words like 'fright', 'terror' and 'bewildered', applied equally to killer and victim.

"I done another bad thing."

Although Lennie says he has done another 'bad thing', we are never sure that he fully grasps its significance. Or is it that he does know the difference between right and wrong but is unaware of the effects of his own great

Lennie

strength? Lennie is far more worried that what he has done will make George cross. Steinbeck uses the word 'pawed' here to remind you of the animal imagery which always accompanies Lennie and his actions.

More evidence of Lennie's inability to tell 'good' from 'bad' is that he leaves Curley's wife to go and conceal the puppy's body, because he thinks that the evidence of its death will make things worse for him. Lennie has no in-built sense that people are any more important than other animals. Notice how Lennie's neglect has the effect of making the death of Curley's wife even sadder.

'The sun-streaks were high on the wall by now...'

Nature

This lyrical, descriptive passage emphasises the contrast with the violence of the drama that has just taken place. The scene is set at dusk and the sounds which Steinbeck mentions are more distant and harmonious. The dog which comes in reminds the reader of Lennie's lost animal state of 'innocence'. By her death, Curley's wife is also returned to a natural state of innocence from which she had been separated by her discontented ambition. In death she does not present an horrific sight, but is described in an idyllic way.

'As happens sometimes, a moment settled...'

Steinbeck's writing technique is very similar to script-writing for the cinema. We have seen how carefully he constructs settings for each main section of the book and only then introduces the characters. Here he introduces what in a film might be a kind of 'freeze-frame'. This device creates a quiet moment before the turbulence of the conclusion of the story.

Candy discovers the body of Curley's wife

As the action resumes, it is ironic that it should be Candy who enters – since he has been working out more details of the farm, which would of course have been Lennie's salvation. All their hopes are dashed by his discovery of the body. Notice how Steinbeck uses sound to accompany the restarting of the action: the noises get louder, from 'stamped' and 'chinked' to 'stamped and snorted', 'chewed' and 'clashed'.

George worries about what will happen

George

George has been removed from the action for about thirty pages, and now he reappears. This has given Lennie the freedom to behave without George's guiding and restraining hand. George confesses that what has happened is what he feared all along. His thoughts are for Lennie and he hopes that he will be, at worst, put in prison and cared for. You may feel that George's idea might not be the best thing for Lennie, who has been identified from the start with unspoilt naturalness. Perhaps Lennie would never have been safe, even on the 'dream farm'. Candy, who is much more realistic now, says that the ranch-hands, led by Curley, will exact their own kind of brutal justice.

Candy fears that the dream of the farm is now dead

Candy's 'greatest fear' is that the farm is now gone. Because of Curley's wife,

Lennie has sinned and the heaven of the farm will now never be his. The heaven the men dreamed of was to have been a place where black and white and the sick of mind and the sick of body would all be restored to full humanity – a place where all would be made whole and equal.

Dreams

George realises that his own prospects are now no better than those of all the other itinerant workers, with their limited aspirations of cheap sex and gambling. George is quick-witted enough to think of a strategy which will absolve him from blame. Is he being callous here, do you think, or just realistic?

Lennie is "such a nice fella"

Circumstance and the quirks of Lennie's character have brought about this

tragic conclusion. George says that Lennie was never motivated by malice and that the victims are just casualties of his innocence. Candy's bitter attack on Curley's wife hints at her symbolic role – through her action of 'messing things up' he and his friends have lost their 'dream' and the chance of a new life. Are these judgements of Lennie and of Curley's wife fair?

Lennie

Slim examines the body of Curley's wife

Slim examines the body and confirms that Curley's wife is dead. Everyone respects his authority as the leader of the group. Even allowing for Curley's emotional reaction, you should still notice that the basis of Slim's authority is a quiet firmness, while Curley's instinct is always towards instant violence.

Carlson becomes excited

The prospect of a man-hunt and the opportunity to use his Luger excites

Carlson, who seems to want to solve all his problems with his gun. His keenness to use his Luger on Lennie reminds us of his former enthusiasm to use it on Candy's dog. Interestingly, it has gone missing. Can you now work out the other reason for George's wanting to get back to the bunkhouse before the body of Curley's wife is discovered by the others?

Violence

'Curley came suddenly to life.'

Curley's response is aggressive, probably because he already has a score to settle with Lennie. Rather than let the law take its course, Curley announces his intention of shooting Lennie in the stomach with a shot-gun. This would lead to a very slow and painful death.

Curley

George sends the men the wrong way

Although he does all he can to get the men to promise that they will take Lennie alive and not harm him, George can tell from the way Curley treats the search as a hunt for an animal, saying he will 'shoot for the guts' by way of revenge, that there would be no hope of Lennie coming out of it alive.

Slim is as perceptive as usual and realises that to catch Lennie alive and lock him up would not really be the answer. He talks about Lennie's capture as if Lennie were a wild animal. Slim seems to be suggesting that the most humane way to treat Lennie would be to kill him.

Section 6

This final section returns to the opening setting. In a way which echoes the shooting of Candy's dog, Lennie has been 'taken outside' by Steinbeck into the natural world where he belongs and where he is to die.

The 'deep green pool of the Salinas River' is the setting for the final action

of the novel, just as it was for its opening. It is useful to compare both of these descriptions. The pastoral calm is still noticeable, but the action of the heron here in swallowing the little water-snake hints at the violence in nature. The silence of the original setting is disturbed here by the 'gust' of the wind and the noise of the leaves, which occurred only at the very end of the opening scene.

Nature

The suggestion is that all life returns to the pool. To get a clearer idea of what is meant, try to imagine how this might look if it were a scene in a film. By ending the novel where it began, Steinbeck brings the action of the book full circle. This gives a feeling of completeness to the story, but does it give you the same feeling about the lives of the characters? We are left with the feeling that they are forever doomed to wander from farm to farm, through season after season, from casual acquaintance to casual acquaintance, endlessly repeating the hopeless cycle of their lives.

Lennie appears, like 'a creeping bear'

The description of Lennie drinking at the pool is in marked contrast to that in the opening section. This time, instead of throwing himself into the water,

Lennie

he drinks as a real wild animal might, cautiously, alert for every sound. His movements resemble those of a bear, including the way he holds his body, allowing him to see the entrance to the watering area. His mind returns to the events of the opening scene, with its conflict between ideas about 'crime' and 'ketchup'. Notice how the animals in the clearing all move away.

'And then from out of Lennie's head…'

Steinbeck again uses a film technique to illustrate the complex nature of

Dreams

Lennie's mentality. His guilt and its consequences are played out in a scene between Aunt Clara (his former guardian) and himself. Aunt Clara is the character of George and says what George would say – although, interestingly, not with his voice. Perhaps Lennie has heard this scene over and over again from George. This first vision is concerned with events in the past. Lennie's conscience (if that is what it is) explains in detail how he has sinned.

You should consider why this strange, dreamlike episode is inserted into the final action. You might think it a very original and effective piece of writing by Steinbeck, or you might instead feel that it is out of place, bizarre and confusing. Can you explain why you feel the way you do about Steinbeck's use of this unusual device? Does Lennie's vision (or dream) add to what you already know or feel about him? Does it make Lennie appear more child-like and vulnerable? Would the story's end have been more moving or more happy if this episode had been omitted, do you think?

Lennie's second vision

The appearance of the giant rabbit is to do with Lennie's fear for the future.

Dreams

The rabbit is a symbol of a time of peace in quiet and natural surroundings, both in the past of childhood (toy rabbits) and in the future of the 'dream farm'. Lennie tells himself that this dream has been shattered by events. He seems to be gaining some grasp of the implications of what has happened although he has to conjure up imaginary beings to explain it to him. This device gives you an insight not only into *what* Lennie thinks, but also the way he thinks.

George arrives as the sun sets

This passage – which begins: 'Only the topmost ridges were in sun now' – is almost identical to a section near the start of the book, except that this time the distant sounds of men are no longer incidental and unimportant, but indicate the whereabouts of the hunting-party. To reassure Lennie, George

George

moves through familiar exchanges to a point where they begin to talk once more about how they have each other for support and companionship. Steinbeck conveys George's anguish with light touches here and there, using words and phrases like 'he said woodenly', 'quiet for a moment', 'shakily'. George also speaks to Lennie calmly and quietly, without his usual outbursts, calling him by his name instead of the more usual 'crazy bastard' and 'son-of-a-bitch', which he uses when he is angry. George has rarely been as gentle as this with Lennie. On which other occasions does he treat him with equal consideration?

The hunting-party approaches

As the hunting-party draws nearer, the 'dream farm' takes on the characteristics

Dreams

of heaven and becomes a haven where Lennie will find peace. George has stolen Carlson's Luger and has come prepared for this final act of friendship. He asks Lennie to remove his hat, thus exposing the back of his head to the bullet in the same place Carlson used with Candy's dog. Dreaming of the future, Lennie dies happily and unsuspectingly.

Steinbeck creates a parallel not only between the shooting of Candy's dog and of Lennie, but also between the emotions which motivate the killings. George ends up by killing Lennie, Lennie has killed Curley's wife, and Carlson killed Candy's dog. All three killers are motivated by a kind of affection, understanding, sense of 'justice', love or compassion. Are they therefore innocent of evil motives?

The final duologue between George and Lennie (with the simple narration of preparations for shooting) is the most moving section of the novel and one which you need to know well: for essays about hope, relationships, victims (question 3, page 63), and much else.

Lennie is killed

Violence

The consequences for Lennie are that – as George has just been saying – there 'Ain't gonna be no more trouble. Nobody gonna hurt nobody nor steal from 'em'. These things would, of course, have been the rewards they were hoping for from their 'dream farm'. Notice the heavy irony in Lennie's urgings to George to 'do it now'.

You will remember that Candy said that he 'ought to of shot that dog myself, George. I shouldn't ought to of let no stranger shoot my dog.' This is probably the main reason why George decides that he should be the one to shoot Lennie, but he may also be protecting him from the treatment he would receive at Curley's hands if he were to find him first.

Nuestra Senora de Soledad

The story is the tale of how simple-minded Lennie has to be sacrificed by his loyal friend George, but it is much more subtle, less straightforward, than that suggests. For example, many Californian place-names have their origin in the Spanish language, and Soledad is an abbreviation of 'Nuestra Senora de Soledad' which means 'Our Lady of Loneliness'. The name refers to the mother of Christ, especially during that part of her life between Good Friday and the Resurrection (Easter Sunday). Think about the significance of the fact that the story in *Of Mice and Men* begins late on a Friday afternoon and ends here, with Lennie's death, on the following Sunday.

George's dream

Throughout the novel George has seemed torn between a genuine affection for Lennie and a desire to be free of a troublesome and inconvenient burden. When he shoots Lennie, George abandons the dream of the farm and accepts the lonely independence and endless games of solitaire 'I'll set in some pool-room till ever'body goes home.'

Nature   The itinerant workers do not exist in the state of innocence and purity which we see described in the natural world. They seem condemned forever to wander in search of their greatest desire – their heaven – their home. Theirs seems to be a world full of senseless violence in which, eventually, death comes to mice and men alike.

Slim understands what George has done and why. He also seems to sense what it has cost George. In contrast, Carlson's question – the final words in the book – summarise the harsh world in which characters like him and Curley live – a world of callousness and brutality. They are unable to understand the world of George and Slim, because they cannot see the basis upon which it is built. Curley and Carlson are not even aware of their own loneliness.

Steinbeck chooses a down-beat ending, closing with Carlson's lack of understanding, not the tragedy or George's arrest or new hope for George. When writing on this novel you are often expected to think for yourself what meaning lies under the simple surface.

About the ending

Do you think that *Of Mice And Men* is mostly a hopeful or a tragic story? Consider whether you feel that the ending of the story was inevitable or whether it might have been possible for George and Lennie to have succeeded in owning their own farm. Does the book offer any redeeming or hopeful view of the itinerants' relationships with each other? Think about whether Steinbeck offers any future for them or any possibility of happiness.

■ Self-test questions Sections 3–6

Uncover the plot

Delete two of the three alternatives given, to find the correct plot. Beware possible misconceptions and muddles

George thanks Slim for giving Lennie one of his puppies, and tells Slim what happened at the pool/in Weed/in the barn. With the tacit permission/disapproval/scorn of Slim, Carlson shoots Candy's old dog. While Curley is out in the barn accusing Lennie/George/Slim of 'messing' with his wife, George and Lennie tell Whit/Candy/Crooks that they are planning to buy a plot of land that George has seen; Candy offers to swamp the farm/tend the rabbits/put up some money towards it if they will include them. Curley returns, mistakes Lennie's smile of delight at the new developments/his puppy/Curley's wife for derision, and picks a fight with him. At George's command, Lennie crushes Curley's hand. All the men go into town/to bed/to work except for Crooks, Lennie and Candy, who meet in Crooks' room to talk. They are interrupted by Curley's wife, who shows special interest in Crooks/Lennie/Candy when she guesses that it was he who hurt Curley's hand. Later that night/in the morning/the following afternoon she finds Lennie in the barn, grieving for the puppy he has inadvertently killed. Without her permission/at her invitation/without warning, Lennie touches her hair; she panics and Lennie, terrified by her silence/tears/screams, breaks her neck. Remembering George's instructions, Lennie returns to the north/Weed/the pool. Curley/George/Candy discovers the body and realises their dream is over; he fetches George, who sends the other men the wrong way/after Lennie/to Soledad while he goes to find Lennie. While Lennie has nightmares/begs George's forgiveness/looks the other way, visualising their dream farm, George shoots him with Carlson's gun.

Who? What? Why? When? Where? How?

1 What does Slim say he has hardly ever seen?
2 How did George and Lennie escape the lynch mob in Weed?
3 Why does Whit show Slim the magazine, and what do you think the magazine represents for the men?
4 What is the 'usual thing' that Whit and the other men do each Saturday night; does George agree to join in with them?
5 Why does George's voice grow 'warmer' when he is telling Lennie about the farm?
6 Who says that he wishes someone would shoot him when he is old/crippled? (Be careful: do more than one of the men say this?)

7   Who persuades Curley not to tell his father how his hand was really crushed, and how?
8   Why do you think Crooks suggests to Lennie that George might not come back?
9   What is Curley's wife's dream, and why is she so keen to 'talk' to Lennie?
10   Why does George go back to the bunk-house after finding the body? Does he tell Candy the whole truth here?

Who is this?

1   Who has 'calm, God-like eyes'?
2   Who 'walked heavily on his heels, as though he carried the invisible grain bag'?
3   Who has got 'yella-jackets in his drawers', and what does that mean?
4   Who 'had thin, pain-tightened lips which were lighter than his face'?
5   Whose eyes 'centred and grew quiet and mad'?
6   Who 'never gets to heaven and… never gets no land'?
7   Who sat 'perfectly still, his eyes averted, everything that might be hurt drawn in'?
8   Whose words 'tumbled out in a passion of communication, as though she hurried before her listener could be taken away'?
9   Who 'wore thick bull's-eye glasses' and a 'huge gingham apron with pockets' and was 'starched and clean'?

General questions

1   The story ends where – for us – it began, at the pool: if you compare the two descriptions of the pool, however, there are several differences.
     (a) Name THREE of the differences.
     (b) Why do you think the author uses this technique?
2   The message at the end of the novel seems to be that aspirations are doomed, that the world is full of senseless violence, and that the fate of man is loneliness and death. Does anything temper the harshness of this message?
3   Do you agree with what George does? Consider the alternatives, and their implications.
4   What technique does Steinbeck use to convey Lennie's state of mind as he waits for George at the pool? What effect(s) does it achieve?
5   Find the quotation that expresses George's ideal world. Does it seem possible to achieve, within the context of this novel?
6   What is the significance of the last line of the novel?

How to write an examination essay

Most of you will be studying *Of Mice and Men* as a set text for your formal examination. This section gives you some guidelines on how to approach an examination essay and also considers three possible subjects.

Before you start writing

- The first essential is thorough revision. It is important that you realise that even Open Book examinations require close textual knowledge. You will have time to look up quotations and references, but *only if you know where to look*.

- Read the questions very carefully, both to choose the best one and to take note of exactly what you are asked to do. Do not answer the question you *imagine or hope* has been set, or repeat the practice essay you wrote earlier on a *similar but slightly different* subject.

- Identify all the key words in the question that mention characters, events and themes, and instructions as to what to do, e.g. compare, contrast, comment, explore, explain, etc. It is very unlikely that simple retelling of the story will gain you much credit.

- Look at the each of points you have identified and jot down what you are going to write about each.

- Decide in what order you are going to deal with the main points. Number them in sequence. This is a matter of choice, but do not use chronological unless you have a good reason to.

Writing the essay

- The first sentences are important. Try to summarise your response to the question so the examiner has some idea of how you plan to approach it. Do not begin, 'George and Lennie got off the bus four miles from the ranch and had to walk...' A good beginning on the relationship between George and Lennie might be, 'The unique and dangerously fragile relationship between George and Lennie, based on mutual dependence, is established in the first section of the novel, with the incidents of the dead mouse and the ketchup, hints of events in Weed and dreams of rabbits.' Jump straight into your argument; do not waste time at the start. A personal response is rewarded, but you must always answer the question – as you write your essay, refer back to your list of points.

- Answer *all of the question*. Many students spend all their time answering just one part of a question and ignoring the rest. This prevents you gaining marks for the parts left out. In the same way, failing to answer enough questions on the examination is a waste of marks which can always be gained most easily at the start of an answer.

- There is no 'correct' length for an essay. What you must do is to spend the full time usefully in answering all parts of the question (spending longer than the allocated time by more than a few minutes is dangerous). Some people write faster than others, but they don't always get the best marks!

- Take care with presentation, spelling and punctuation. It is generally unwise to use slang or contractions (e.g. 'they've' for 'they have').

- Use quotation or paraphrase when it is relevant and contributes to the quality and clarity of your answer. References to events often do not need quotation, but the exact words of such things as George and Lennie's dream of the farm or some of Steinbeck's natural descriptions would be valuable. *Extended* quotations are usually unhelpful and padding is a complete waste of time

Example questions

Below are three examples of the kind of questions you may expect in your exam. An *outline* of a model answer has been supplied for each question. You will find it useful to write full-length versions of these plans, incorporating references from the text to back up the ideas.

1 *It has been said that* Of Mice and Men *is sad but not entirely pessimistic. Do you feel that John Steinbeck shows any hope and optimism about life? Explain your reasons.*

(*NEAB specimen question*)

- First of all you need to be sure that you know the difference between 'sad' and 'pessimistic'. 'Sad' refers to a mood, but 'pessimistic' refers to an attitude: the belief that things will not get better and the lack of hope for the future. The other word which has to be noted closely is 'explain': you must be able to say *why* you find or do not find optimism in *Of Mice and Men.*

- Before starting you must decide whether the novel is totally pessimistic. If you think it is, you will still need to consider some of the points we are going to deal with, even if only to dismiss them.

- In terms of organising the essay, you could start either by explaining the difference between 'sad' and 'pessimistic' or by proving that it is, indeed, sad. This is not at all difficult and does not need to be done at length, but it is a necessary part of the essay.

- The main part of the essay considers whether *Of Mice and Men* is pessimistic. In some ways it is. You should be able to prove that there is no hint that things will improve in terms of prosperity or conditions. You will also find plenty of intolerant and unhelpful people in the novel. You will be able to show dreams crushed by reality.

- However, there are signs that Steinbeck believes that the world has the potential to be a better place and you could divide these into three sections.

- The first and most important is human nature. There are unpleasant people, but there are also those who show the nobility of human nature. You should explain in detail, with extensive quotation and example, that the relationship between George and Lennie and the character of Slim are signs of hope for humanity.

- Secondly, dreams are not presented as hopeless. Perhaps those of Curley's wife never had a chance, but part of the sadness comes from how near George and Lennie get to their dream before tragedy strikes. Human beings will go on dreaming dreams and a few will come true. Explain the mixture of dream and practical reality with which George nearly finds the earthly paradise.

- Thirdly, and more difficult to argue (much quotation needed), Steinbeck finds too much joy in the natural world for the book to be purely pessimistic.

- For your conclusion you could go back to the title and the word 'entirely'. In finding some hope, you are not saying it is a purely optimistic novel, but not *entirely* pessimistic either.

2 *Characters have different ideas in* Of Mice and Men *about:*
   freedom,
   responsibility,
   caring for others,
   and work.
Choose **two** *characters and compare their ideas about each of these. Which of these two characters do you have the more sympathy for, and why?*

(NEAB specimen question)

- This is a very straightforward essay because the title tells you exactly what you must do. However, it is also one where you must be careful to do everything that is asked of you. Reading the question carefully is always very important; here it is absolutely vital.

- First of all you must make sure you do the number of things asked for: consider *four* aspects (given in the question) of *two* characters (chosen by yourself). Then note the key word: *compare*. You must not just write about Candy's views on all four subjects, then about Slim's views on them. You must write that, whereas Slim's idea of freedom is one thing, Candy's is something different (or the same, depending on what you think). Finally, you must not neglect the last section: which of the two do you sympathise with more?

- The next important stage is selecting your two characters. They should be different enough to make interesting contrasts: I would not recommend George and Lennie, for instance, or Candy and Crooks, or the Boss and Curley. In the comments that follow I shall consider George and Curley.

- You could well follow the obvious essay plan for this: an opening paragraph on who the two people are, their different backgrounds, etc, four sections making comparisons on the four themes, and a conclusion about your sympathy for one or the other.

- You can surely find plenty of evidence for the actual contrasts, but also try to find an ongoing link. That could be the fact that George's thinking is dominated by his relationship with Lennie, Curley's by his belief in his own importance and superiority to the ranch-hands. So George pursues freedom via a place of their own for him and Lennie, feels the responsibility of caring for Lennie, etc, but Curley sees all these in terms of authority: trying to limit his wife's freedom, etc. Even on the subject of work (where their views may be most similar) Curley's high-heeled boots mark a difference.

- Remember that sympathy means sharing the views and feelings of somebody, not feeling sorry for him/her. You will probably sympathise more with George, and probably you will find that one of your main reasons for this is that he displays much more human sympathy than Curley.

3 *The title of* Of Mice and Men *suggests that it is about people whose plans never work out as they wish. In fact, many of the characters in the novel can be seen as victims of society. Give an account of the different types of suffering presented in the novel and consider Steinbeck's attitude to the victims.*

- Though this is again fairly straightforward, telling you what to do, it again requires care to follow instructions exactly. First of all you are not given a specific number of characters, and before you start you need to make notes on just who are the victims. Secondly, though this title says 'Give an account', it is not an account of events or characters, but of different types of suffering, so you must work out what makes these people victims. Thirdly, do not miss the last part of the question: Steinbeck's attitude.

- Your list of victims is important as preparation for the essay: Lennie most obviously; George in his relationship with Lennie; Curley's wife; Candy and Crooks are all clearly victims, but you could also make a case for Curley, Carlson and Whit.

- You can take the various categories in any order you like: the order here does not indicate preference. There are the economic victims, the people who earn too little to make anything of their lives. This applies to almost all the characters, though not the Boss or Curley, and it is difficult to see Slim as any kind of victim.

- Perhaps the most important group is the cripples: Crooks and Candy (plus his dog) physically, Lennie mentally. Finding copious evidence for this is fairly easy.

- Most of the characters have no satisfactory private lives. Few are married and those that are suffer by it. Curley is a victim of his marriage just as his wife is.

- A number of characters are victims of violence: Lennie is a victim of Curley's violence, Curley and Curley's wife victims of Lennie's (accidental) violence.

- A further category which relates to many of the characters contains those whose dreams are cruelly crushed, notably Curley's wife and all those who dream of the farm.

- Again, as in the previous essay, the last part of the question provides a neat concluding paragraph. Steinbeck's attitude is clearly sympathetic, but how can you prove this? Some of his descriptions convey sympathy, certainly, but above all several of the victims show nobility of character and most of them dream dreams that offer an alternative view of their fate. Steinbeck gives them an audience for their dreams and even Curley's wife is not simply foolish and flirtatious.

How to write a coursework essay

Most of you are unlikely to have to write a coursework essay on *Of Mice and Men*, but you may wish to use the book as the twentieth-century comparison to pre-twentieth-century fiction in a Wide Reading assignment. If you do so, you should bear the following points in mind.

- There must be a *specific* ground for comparison. The comparison should be made throughout the essay, not necessarily in the same sentence, but at least in adjacent paragraphs.

- You can use *Of Mice and Men* with a very different novel or short story, but there must be one definite respect (or more than one) in which you can find similarities or differences or both.

- For example, if you are writing on a Thomas Hardy novel or short story, the theme of the agricultural poor can offer common ground. George and Lennie share common ground with Michael Henchard (at the beginning of *The Mayor of Casterbridge*) or Tess, wandering in search of work with a private life that has collapsed into disaster. At the same time you can find comparisons and contrasts in the world of work.

- Hardy is one of several novelists you could choose for their use of tragedy: like Steinbeck, Hardy often deals with the tragedies of the harmless and the innocent.

- Unlikely as it may seem, if you are writing about Mary Shelley's *Frankenstein*, *Of Mice and Men* could give you a useful comparison in the central characters' relationships to one another: like Frankenstein, George tries to impose control on a character of enormous power and limited understanding, in both cases an oddly sympathetic figure. In both novels the control fails, with tragic results.

- The use of pathos in *Of Mice and Men* could provide an acceptable comparison with Dickens, who also often wrote of the damaged and the helpless (many children in the latter category): in particular, the George/Lennie relationship could provide a good comparison with Nicholas Nickleby and Smike. There are contrasts, of course, particularly the social background and Dickens' distinctly more sentimental approach and greater range of characterisation.

- It is essential to make reference to the historical, social and cultural background of the texts. This will not provide a problem because the background to *Of Mice and Men* is so different from any pre-twentieth-century novel: you will need to explain this anyway and by doing so will fulfil the requirement.

With any coursework essay (whether a comparison or a study of one text) there are certain considerations always to be borne in mind:

- It is essential that you show considerable evidence of textual knowledge even if the essay has a strong creative element.

- In an analytical essays the *most important* consideration is that you must develop an argument or explain a point of view throughout. Careful advance preparation will aid you in organising your theme or argument: making notes on the material, putting these notes in order, then working through two or three drafts of the essay. Thus you should be able to make a decision on what each paragraph is about, as far as possible signalling this to the reader in the opening sentence, often called a *topic sentence* because it states the topic of the paragraph.

- If you are writing an imaginative/creative essay, the *first essential* is to reveal throughout your factual knowledge of the text and a soundly based interpretation of it. Mere imagination will not gain credit in textual study for GCSE English Literature.

- In terms of length of essay, do bear in mind that it is only one of several pieces of coursework and there is no need for a 5,000 word blockbuster. Many essays will exceed 1,000 words, but by how much depends on the material you wish to present and the advice of your teacher.

Self-test answers Section 1

Uncover the plot
Delete two of the three alternatives given, to find the correct plot. Beware possible misconceptions and muddles.

Two itinerant farm hands, George and Lennie, camp beside a natural pool in a valley before travelling on to a nearby ranch to find work. It becomes clear that George – small and quick-witted – is responsible for the huge and child-like Lennie, and that the two men have had to leave the town of Weed because Lennie unwittingly frightened a girl there. George expresses his resentment at having to look after Lennie, but when Lennie offers to leave him, he regrets his meanness. We learn that Lennie has a passion for 'petting' pretty things, especially small animals, unaware of his own dangerous strength. George describes their dream of buying a house; he tells Lennie to return to the pool if he should get into any trouble.

Who? Why? What? When? Where? How?
1 In a valley at the foot of the Gabilan mountains, a few miles south of Soledad
2 A path, an ash-pile, and a sycamore tree branch worn smooth by men sitting on it
3 It is only safe to drink running water; Lennie has been sick before from drinking 'still' water
4 He imitates George's actions exactly
5 A mouse; his work card
6 Lennie's Aunt Clara
7 Lennie frightened a girl there, and the two men were chased out of town
8 They have each other, so they are not lonely; they have a 'future' that consists of more than sitting in bars
9 They plan to buy a house and some land of their own; they need a 'jack' or 'stake' (enough money to put down a deposit)
10 In case the boss sees that Lennie is 'crazy', and refuses to give them work

Who is this?
1 George
2 Lennie
3 Lennie
4 A water snake
5 The girl Lennie frightened in Weed
6 Ranch workers
7 George and Lennie; they will eat and sell the produce that they grow – it will be their livelihood

Who said that?
1 George, of Lennie; he knows Lennie has gone to find the mouse, and pities him for his childish need for things to 'pet'
2 George
3 Lennie; of George's description of their dream future; Lennie enjoys the story as a child enjoys a fairytale at bedtime, and anyway would not be capable of telling it – he cannot even remember where they are going the following day

A complicated friendship
1 Even at this early stage in the book, before either character has spoken or even been described, one of the men is the leader and the other subservient to him. Note that Lennie follows George 'even in the open'

2   George knows that Lennie is incapable of keeping anything safe – indeed, of looking after himself at all – and so has kept his work card safe for him. In doing so he is acting like a father or an older brother, taking responsibility for Lennie

3   Like a child, Lennie is easily upset by the loss of his mouse. George is at once frustrated that a grown man should react in this way, and sorry to have upset his friend. He shows affection for Lennie, expressing it both verbally and physically

4   Lennie has a simple cunning that allows him to manipulate ('put something over') George. This cunning is expressed in terms reminiscent of wild animals ('bait', 'sensing' an advantage): like theirs, Lennie's intelligence is basic. He knows that the relationship is not one-sided, and that George needs him. What does George need Lennie for? Perhaps for physical protection and self-esteem – and most of all for company?

5   George and Lennie share the dream, and take it in turns to 'tell' it. The dream bonds them together; unlike other ranch workers, they care for and protect each other and hope to have a future together. Lennie delights in their dream as a child delights in a story, repeating things word for word, even though he seems barely to understand their meaning

Important images

1   The stillness of a hot summer evening; the harmony, beauty, peace and innocence of nature at the pool (shortly to be interrupted by the men's footsteps). Do you think it is coincidence that rabbits are amongst the creatures mentioned?

2   There are two important images here. Lennie's hand is a 'big paw'; this creates an impression of his size, as well as likening its owner to a large animal (suggesting both brute strength and animal-like innocence). Note that Lennie is linked with horses, bears, terriers and coyotes in this section. The ripples in the water reappear a few pages later as the carp comes up for air; they perhaps suggest hidden depths in Lennie, as well as in the pool, and the widening repercussions of Lennie's child-like behaviour

3   The powerful beauty of the scenery surrounding the two men; the majesty of the mountains. Steinbeck's style evokes immediacy and detail (the word 'flamed' creates both the intensity of the light and its movement)

4   The mysterious depths of the pool, in which unknown and unseen things live; perhaps there is a suggestion of a future that is dark and unknown

5   Lennie's subservience and fearful respect of George; his reluctance is almost described as a stage direction in a play – we are in no doubt as to his exact actions and manner

Self-test answers section 2

Uncover the plot
Delete two of the three alternatives given, to find the correct plot. Beware possible misconceptions and muddles.

George and Lennie arrive at the ranch. They are given bunks by Candy, the swamper, and signed up by the boss. The boss is angry that they arrived too late for the morning's work, and suspicious of George's protectiveness of Lennie. Curley, the boss' son, is antagonistic towards the new men, especially Lennie; they learn from Candy that Curley has recently married a 'tart'. The whole set-up scares George, who warns Lennie to have nothing to do with Curley. The other ranch hands return from work. Slim is very friendly; Carlson is more concerned with shooting Candy's old dog, and asks Slim to give Candy one of his puppies to raise. In the midst of Lennie's excitement at the possibility of owning a pup, Curley returns in search of his errant wife.

Who? What? Why? When? Where? How?

1   The blacksmith who had George's bunk before him; a very nice and clean man; to calm George down when he thinks that his bunk is infested
2   Neatly and carefully; slowly
3   10 miles; 4–5 miles (in the first section George says that the bus driver dropped them 'at least' 4 miles away from the pool, and the pool is close to the ranch)
4   Small; because Lennie is huge
5   Of taking Lennie's pay away from him; George won't let Lennie speak for himself
6   To keep his hand soft for his wife
7   After they have made a few dollars (as soon as possible); at once
8   The man in charge of a team of mules, capable of controlling up to 20 animals with only one line to the leaders of the team
9   The mother couldn't feed all of the puppies
10 The dog smells (this is Carlson's main concern, but he does point out that the dog is in pain and 'no good to himself')

Who is this?

1   The stable-buck
2   The boss
3   Lennie
4   Candy's old dog
5   A 'guy on a ranch'
6   Curley's
7   Curley
8   Curley's wife
9   Curley's wife, as she appears in the bunk-house
10 Slim's

Who's in charge?

1   Candy, George, then Lennie. Candy, with the advantage of familiarity with his surroundings, would naturally go first to show the new men the way; as in the first section, Lennie follows George. Compare Carlson allowing Slim to go out to lunch before him
2   He doesn't 'give a damn'. Crooks is well read and educated and – particularly as a black man in 1930s America – is likely to understand the futility and even the danger of standing up to the boss
3   He is antagonistic and aggressive. His dress is black (the stereotyped 'bad man') and severe; he wears spurs and heels to show that he is superior to the labourers
4   In not permitting Lennie to speak, George arouses the boss' suspicion and irritation. Perhaps George is over-defensive and over-protective – and yet can we understand why he cannot rely on Lennie to say the right thing. George then vents his anger on Lennie, very harshly; this, coupled with his explosion when Lennie pronounces Curley's wife 'purty', suggests that Lennie is a scapegoat for George's frustration when things are not going to plan

5   Any authority that Curley has is achieved through bullying, violence and brutality. No one respects him, but because he is the boss' son they cannot stand up to him for fear of losing their job. Curley wears high heels like his father – perhaps as much because he is small as to differentiate himself from the other workers

6   Slim has natural authority. His skill, his dignity and his 'understanding beyond thought' command respect and even awe; he does not need to use force, cruelty or aggression. Despite his capabilities, he does not try to put himself above the others. He is described as having 'majesty', 'gravity', 'profound quiet', 'understanding beyond thought'; he is 'gentle', 'kindly' and 'friendly'

Sunshine shapes

1   'At about ten o'clock in the morning the sun threw a bright dust-laden bar through one of the side windows, and in and out of the beam flies shot like rushing stars'

2   'The sun square was on the floor now, and the flies whipped through it like sparks.'

3   'The sunshine lay in a thin line under the window.'

The movement of the sun outside creates a sense of time passing and of life going on outside the bunk-house. The atmosphere in the bunk-house is generally dark ('dusk'), foreshadowing the 'trouble' that is to come and the two men's feelings that it is 'mean' at the ranch

Background noise

Choose from: 'jingling harness'; 'croak of heavy-laden axles'; the call of 'Stable Buck!'; 'hooves on hard ground'; 'drag of brakes'; 'jingle of trace chains'; men calling; the ring of the triangle; the rattle of dishes.

These noises separate George and Lennie, and the action/dialogue within the bunk-house, from the outside – life goes on as normal outside, as their story unfolds. They provide a wider setting and context for the action, as well as emphasising the hard work confronting the ranch workers. Coupled with the sunlight outside and the 'dusk' inside the bunk-house, the noises help to create a sense of threat. Think about how voices and footsteps interrupted the stillness and peace of the natural world of the pool in Section 1

■ Self-test answers sections 3–6

Uncover the plot

Delete two of the three alternatives given, to find the correct plot. Beware possible misconceptions and muddles

George thanks Slim for giving Lennie one of his puppies, and tells Slim what happened in Weed. With the tacit permission of Slim, Carlson shoots Candy's old dog. While Curley is out in the barn accusing Slim of 'messing' with his wife, George and Lennie tell Candy that they are planning to buy a plot of land that George has seen; Candy offers to put up some money towards it if they will include them. Curley returns, mistakes Lennie's smile of delight at the new developments for derision, and picks a fight with him. At George's command, Lennie crushes Curley's hand. All the men go into town except for Crooks, Lennie and Candy, who meet in Crooks' room to talk. They are interrupted by Curley's wife, who shows special interest in Lennie when she guesses that it was he who hurt Curley's hand. The following afternoon she finds Lennie in the barn, grieving for the puppy he has inadvertently killed. At her invitation, Lennie touches her hair; she panics and Lennie, terrified by her screams, breaks her neck. Remembering George's instructions, Lennie returns to the pool. Candy discovers the body and realises their dream is over; he fetches George, who sends the other men the wrong way while he goes to find Lennie. While Lennie looks the other way, visualising their dream farm, George shoots him with Carlson's gun.

Who? What? Why? When? Where? How?
1   Two men travelling together
2   They hid in an irrigation ditch
3   There is a letter in it from a man who used to work with them at the ranch; glamour, perhaps, and a life that is very different from the one they are living
4   Go to Susy's place, a bar and brothel; George agrees to visit the place, but not to spend his and Lennie's stake on having a woman there (a 'flop')
5   He starts to believe in what he is saying, and to visualise the details
6   Both Slim and Candy
7   Slim; by saying that Curley will become a laughing stock if the truth gets out
8   Crooks is envious because the two men have each other's companionship, and bitter because of how he is treated by other men
9   To be in the movies, wear nice clothes and be the centre of attention; she too is very lonely, because she has to stay in the house and talk only to Curley
10 He tells Candy that he doesn't want to be seen with the body, because the other men might think he played a part in the girl's death; however, we realise later that he has already decided to shoot Lennie, and has gone to the bunk-house to take Carlson's gun

Who is this?
1   Slim
2   Whit
3   Curley; the equivalent of 'ants in his pants'
4   Crooks
5   Lennie's, when he thinks George is threatened
6   'Nobody'
7   Crooks, before the onslaught of Curley's wife
8   Curley's wife's
9   Lennie's Aunt Clara (or rather Lennie's 'vision' of her)

General questions
1   (a) Choose from: the water-snake is eaten by the heron; a gust of wind blows (in the first section all is still, until the very end of the 'scene'); Lennie drinks carefully and warily, instead of 'snorting like a horse'; the sounds of men calling are not incidental, but signify the approach of the hunting party
    (b) To give the story a shape and a structure, so that things are 'come full circle' (all life returns to the universal pool)
2   Consider Slim: the very existence of a Slim in a world of Curleys and Carlsons is perhaps hopeful. Consider also that George's act was not one of cruelty but rather one of kindness and of selflessness – how does George envisage his life without Lennie?
3   Consider the death that Lennie would have suffered at Curley's hands ('Shoot for his guts'), or the life he would have had locked up (as Slim says, strapped down in a cage). Could Lennie have continued as he was doing, without finally getting into trouble that George could not cure?
4   A dream-like (or nightmare-like) sequence, in which – like thought bubbles – Aunt Clara and then a giant rabbit 'come out of Lennie's head'. Do you find this reminiscent of film/movie techniques (think of the 'moment' in the barn

after the death of Curley's wife, which is just like a movie still). Lennie seems even more vulnerable and child-like as he wrestles out loud with his conscience and his worst fears, with some grasp of the implications of what has happened

5   'Ain't gonna be no more trouble. Nobody gonna hurt nobody nor steal from 'em.' The novel's message is very bleak: there is little to suggest that prejudice, oppression and cruelty can be overcome

6   Unlike Slim, Carlson and Curley are completely incapable of appreciating what George's action has cost him; insensitive and without insight, they are unaware of their own loneliness and shortcomings